BIRDS OF A FEATHER

Birds of a Feather

UNPUBLISHED LETTERS OF
W. H. HUDSON

EDITED AND INTRODUCED BY DENNIS SHRUBSALL

WITH WOOD ENGRAVINGS BY MARCUS BEAVEN

Moonraker Press

Contents

WOOD ENGRAVINGS: *Title page, 'Bottle' Tit's nest; p. 17, Dartford Warbler; p. 23, Ring Ouzel; p. 31, Sparrow Hawk; p. 41, Stone Curlew; p. 47, Bittern; p. 57, Golden Oriole; p. 67, Wheatear; p. 79, Cirl Bunting; p. 89, Crossbill; p. 99, Pintail.*

'Straight between them ran the pathway,
Never grew the grass upon it;
Singing birds, that utter falsehoods,
Story-tellers, mischief-makers,
Found no eager ear to listen,
Could not breed ill-will between them,
For they kept each other's counsel,
Spake with naked hearts together . . .

HENRY WADSWORTH LONGFELLOW

Introduction

It is perhaps unique to find someone who, though not born and raised in England, has written so intimately and sensitively about the English countryside that he has become established among the immortals of English countryside writers. But this is true of William Henry Hudson who was born in Argentina in 1841 of American parents, and raised on their *estancia* – or ranch – on the great cattle- and sheep-grazing plain of South America, the pampas. However, Englishmen were among his forebears, and perhaps due to this, to contact with English settlers in Argentina, to books read in his youth, and to an association with the Zoological Society of London, he left South America for England in 1874: and here he remained for the rest of his long life – for despite the handicap of a weak heart resulting from a serious illness in his youth, he lived until he was 81 years old.

Much of Hudson's 33 years in South America had been spent adventurously in the open air, and he acquired an extensive knowledge of the birds and other creatures of the districts in which he lived and travelled. From early boyhood he was preoccupied with nature, and what he lacked in formal tuition was more than compensated by wide reading, discussions and extensive field experience. During 1869 and 1870 he wrote some letters about the birds of the Province of Buenos Aires to the Zoological Society of London which published them in its 'Proceedings'.[1] Later, while living in England, he wrote a number of books about Argentina such as *The Naturalist in La Plata*,[2] *Idle Days in Patagonia*[3] and *Birds of La Plata*,[4] and was elected a Fellow of the Society.

Hudson described himself, not merely as a naturalist, but as a 'Field Naturalist', who, he said, 'is an observer of everything he sees – from a man to an ant or a plant'.[5] He also drew a distinction between those who, as he put it, 'weigh, count, measure and dissect for purposes of identification, classification and what not',[6] and the field naturalist who, he said, must see the creature 'undivested of life or liberty or of anything belonging to it . . . in the midst of the nature in which it harmoniously moves and has its being'.[7] Thus, in England as in South America, his workshop was not the laboratory, the lecture-room or the library, but the countryside: and the tools of his trade were not instruments of research but his eyes – often assisted by binoculars – and his legs, sometimes walking and sometimes pedalling his bicycle. His *modus operandi* was observing life first-hand, birds particularly, but not neglecting mammals, reptiles, insects, plants, trees, grass, and even men and women: and what is more, he discerned them with the eyes and the mind of a poet.

But, you will say, surely as a writer his writing implements were his tools too? And, of course, you are right, but mostly they were secondary only. To observe nature was to be alive and fulfilled: he wrote about it to give to ordinary people a glimpse of its wonder and poetry divorced from the academic straightjacket of biology and statistics, and as a means of obtaining the simple necessities of his life.

Success in its worldly connotation did not come to Hudson until late in life, and when it did he was indifferent to it and to the money which it brought him. It was ironic that money came to him when he least needed it. His first 25 years in England were years of acute and unaccustomed poverty. Lack of money severely restricted both the frequency and duration of the countryside rambles upon which his work depended; and but for a politician's understanding of the value of his work and the restrictions under which he laboured the world might well have been denied some of his finest nature writings.[8] Relief was given in the form of a Civil List Pension of £150 a year which was granted 'in recognition of the originality of his writings on Natural History'[9] and which enabled him to continue with his work.

In the Spring of 1906 when Edward VII was ruling over a prosperous and influential British Empire, a London actor, John Rudge Harding, took his courage in both hands and wrote to Hudson about Dartford warblers. Though 45 years of age and a keen student of birds for most of his life, Harding understandably could have been a little timid and apprehensive about proffering ornithological information to a well-known naturalist and writer who was also 20 years his senior. But Hudson was grateful for the information and wrote back: it started a correspondence – mostly about birds – which, though intermittent, continued until Hudson's death 16 years later.

At the outbreak of war in 1914 Harding was too old to enlist in the armed forces so he accepted an invitation to join the British Red Cross Society and served in the Auxiliary Home Hospitals Department. Later when the Star and Garter Home for Disabled Sailors and Soldiers was being planned he was appointed its first secretary. Though for 30 years a well-known actor – he had performed with Sir John Hare, the Kendals, Cyril Maude and Fred and Ellen Terry – Harding did not return to the stage after the war. Instead he chose to continue as secretary of the Star and Garter Home, a position which he occupied with distinction until his death at age 70, having been awarded an O.B.E. for his work.

Harding's interest in birds never abated, and a few months before Hudson died he was appointed a member of H.M. Office of Works Committee for Bird Sanctuaries in Royal Parks, and elected to the Council of the Royal Society for the Protection of Birds. He treasured the letters which he had received from Hudson, and carefully preserved them in a leather-bound book which, after his death, came into the possession of his nephew, Sir Harold Harding, who has generously made them available to me.

The remaining letters (or extracts therefrom) which appear in this volume were written by Hudson mainly while rambling about the countryside of Southern England between the years 1896 and 1904. At the beginning of this period Queen Victoria was in the last decade of her reign; Richard Jefferies had been dead for nine years, but Thomas Hardy was alive and writing; cheap wheat and meat imported from abroad had caused an agricultural depression and many farmworkers were leaving the land for the booming manufacturing towns, or to emigrate. It was the golden age of the railways, and the bicycle was fast becoming a popular means of transport; but motor-cars were a rarity, thus the old rural character of the countryside had remained essentially undisturbed and unbesmirched. During these years Hudson was gathering the material for what are probably his three finest English countryside books, *Nature in Downland*[10] devoted to Sussex and especially the South Downs, *A Shepherd's Life*[11] which is set in the South Wiltshire Downs, and *Hampshire Days*.[12]

His correspondents, Mrs Emma Hubbard and Mrs Eliza

Phillips, obviously shared his interest in, and love of, the English countryside and those wild things living and growing in it.

When the first of these letters was written Mrs Hubbard was in her late sixties and Mrs Phillips her early seventies. Both were ladies of position and means with literary backgrounds. Mrs Hubbard, also a talented artist and skilled in the techniques of indexing scientific works, indexed Hudson's book, *Nature in Downland* and drew some of the illustrations for his *Hampshire Days*. When she died in 1905 he wrote to Mrs Phillips, 'Her life of love for everybody and everything was very beautiful'.[13]

Mrs Phillips lived to 93, pre-deceasing Hudson by only six years, and she spent a substantial part of her long life working for the welfare and protection of animals and birds. Like Hudson, she was a devoted and enthusiastic doyen of the Royal Society for the Protection of Birds in which she held a number of offices including those of Vice-President and Chairman of Committee.

Hudson's commitment to the preservation of birds is legend, and he has been cited as one of the five principal champions of wild-bird protection in the England of his day, in which many species were being exterminated to provide embellishments for womens' clothing, stuffed ornaments for the home or delicacies for the dinner table. Except for a few personal bequests he left his entire estate to the Royal Society for the Protection of Birds.

Unlike many public figures of his time Hudson never intended these letters for publication, but having survived their author for over half a century it is unthinkable that they should be allowed to remain merely as collectors' items in libraries, unread and un-enjoyed by all but a few scholars and devotees. If it was possible to ask him about it now perhaps he would say, as in life he once said about another of his letters, 'you may do as you think best, and if you were to print it I should neither approve nor dis-approve'.[14] When writing for publication Hudson worked slowly and meticulously and his daily output was small. His letters, on the other hand, convey the impression that his pen is hastening to keep pace with his thoughts. Sometimes he abbreviated, and I have removed many of these abbreviations, replacing them with complete words. Paragraphing was often ignored, and I have remedied this as I am sure he would have done. He seldom put complete dates on his letters, but fortunately some of these omissions were made good by the recipients. Where they have not, and I have been able to make a reasonable deduction, the assumed date appears in brackets.

These, then, are the letters of a man who spent his life regarding nature, not coldly and dispassionately, but inquisitively and affectionately; and he laboured to protect it and to help others to love it too. In solitary communion with nature and her untamed children in wild places he saw what he loved and loved what he saw. Of his association with his beloved wild birds he once wrote, 'The days – ay, and years – which I have spent in the society of my feathered friends have not, I flatter myself, been so wasted that I cannot small my soul, . . . to bring it within reach of them, and establish some sort of a passage.'[15] Surely he was as the man spoken of by Eliphaz the Temanite in the Book of Job:

> *For thou shalt be in league*
> *with the stones of the field:*
> *and the beasts of the field*
> *shall be at peace with thee.*[16]

Salisbury, Wiltshire   DENNIS SHRUBSALL
1981

ACKNOWLEDGEMENTS

It has been a great privilege to transcribe and edit these letters and I am grateful to Sir Harold Harding, B.Sc., F.C.G.I., D.I.C., F.I.C.E., for allowing me to make use of W. H. Hudson's letters to his uncle, the late J. R. Harding, Esq, O.B.E.; to the Royal Society for the Protection of Birds for Hudson's letters to the late Mesdames E. Hubbard and E. Phillips; and to Philip M. Correll, Esq. for Hudson's charming letter to Elsa.

Again I acknowledge, with grateful thanks, the assistance which I have received from the Salisbury Divisional Library (Wiltshire Library and Museum Service), and in particular from Reference Librarians E. M. Boyle, Esq, A.L.A., and N. R. Goddard, Esq, A.L.A.

My sincere thanks also to I. K. Dawson, Esq, the Librarian of the Royal Society for the Protection of Birds and R. Fish, Esq, the Librarian of the Zoological Society of London for information which they have so kindly provided.

I am grateful also to the Royal Society for the Protection of Birds and to Sir Harold Harding for allowing me to reproduce the photographs on the dust jacket.

PART I

Letters to J. R. Harding

Hudson's opening and closing salutations have been omitted.

The first six letters (14 June 1906 to 19 August 1909) began 'Dear Sir'. The next 16 (9 July 1910 to 10 June [1914]) began 'Dear Mr Harding', with one 'My dear Mr Harding'. Then, *after eight years*, at Hudson's suggestion they dropped formalities, and the remaining letters open with either 'Dear Harding' or 'My dear Harding', (one with 'My dear Rudge Harding').

The closing salutation of the first letter was 'Yours very truly': thereafter Hudson used 'Yours sincerely', sometimes with the addition of 'very'. Once he signed himself 'Yours always'.

I

(14 June 1906 from 40 St Lukes Road, W.[1])

I am obliged to you for telling me of the Dartford Warblers. I thought I would look at the book – *British Birds*[2] – before writing to see just what I had said, but cannot find a copy among my books now. The fact is I did not know much about the bird from personal observation when I wrote that book. I knew more when I wrote *Birds and Man*[3] when I had found the species in four counties. One was in the vicinity of Frencham, where the bird still exists at various points in small colonies, so that it is not strange it should have been discovered near Blackwater. I have failed to find the bird in Berkshire, where it used to be common in one or two localities, but if it had bred for some years at the spot you name, we may look for it again in that county on the borders of Hampshire. I think it is increasing a little now: ten years ago I greatly feared that it was vanishing.

A young Scotch naturalist wrote to me about three weeks ago asking me to advise him as to the best spot in Southern England to see as many species of birds, unknown in Scotland, as he could during his short holiday of eight days. I told him to try Selborne[4] and the country round. He has now given me an account of the birds he found, and among them the Dartford Warbler which he had little expected to see. He found it in the furze bushes on a common close to Frensham Great Pond.

I am always grateful to be told of a new locality of the bird, and always express the hope that it will be told only to those who are known to persons who are anxious to preserve it from the collectors.

2

(13 August 1906 from 40 St Lukes Road, W.)

Thank you for a very interesting letter. Evidently the swifts in that part still keep up the custom of gathering for an afternoon frolic at Selborne.

I do not disbelieve the story of a swallow found hybernating in a rabbit burrow. I am convinced that every year when the swallows migrate a few birds remain and eventually perish of cold and hunger, but that a few do manage to keep alive in a torpid condition until the following Spring. We know of one recent case of two swallows at a country parsonage remaining in that condition in an outhouse through the winter. One died before the Spring, the other revived and was seen flying about the place for many days after.

A few years ago I was staying at Newbury at the end of November, and one day after a cold wet spell the sun shone very strong, and about eleven o'clock a dozen or fifteen swallows made their appearance and spent the day flying up and down in the street in a slow feeble bat-like manner. I believe the warm sun revived them in some hole in which they had been lying. Probably they went back to it towards evening, but I don't suppose that more than a very few of these non-migratory swallows survive the cold season.[5]

It is difficult to believe that all the old stories about swallows being found in holes in banks, etc, had no foundation, but one can imagine how the idea (arose[6]) that swallows took to the water to lay up. The way a migratory flock of swallows dashes down and vanishes in a bed of reeds in a lake or river makes it appear that they had actually gone down into the water. The subject would be a good one for a paper.

———————————————

3

(*1 November 1906 from 40 St Lukes Road, W.*)

Thank you for your letter which is full of interesting observations.

I have not seen a sparrowhawk in the Gardens[7] and did not know about one having been seen there. A few evenings ago I stayed in until it was quite dark in the hope of seeing or hearing an owl, and only on coming out when talking to the keeper at the lodge near the Fountains an owl began hooting and then another at a distance responded. I suppose there are at least two pairs of brown owls as they inhabit clumps of trees a good distance apart.

I have been waiting for the water to be supplied to the lake in St Jame's Park before going there in the evening, and so have not seen the starlings going to roost. I see they have given up the island in the Serpentine as a roosting place.

On most evenings when I am out I see flocks of starlings passing over Kensington Gardens on their way to St James' and Battersea Parks.

For some time past I have been a good deal of the time out of London and so am not very well up in the movements of the London birds.[8] Wood pigeons are still common in the parks but I fancy the number that have gone out of town is greater than the remaining birds. Those that nest at a distance from the parks have all vanished. A pair have nested here, close by, for the last three years: I know those birds pretty well, as the male usually sits on the roof of a bow window over my bedroom and coos his song about four o'clock every morning in Summer.

I am very glad to know you like my *Hampshire Days*[9] so well.

4

(*5 July 1907 from 40 St Lukes Road, W.*)

The snipe is certainly a puzzling bird but I should say the note
you describe was uttered by the female. At all events I took it for
a call of the female when I heard it and my reason for doing so was
because it resembles the female call in another species of snipe –
Gallinago paraguaiæ of South America which I used to observe.
What I observed often was this: when the birds (the males I
supposed) were up in the air performing just as the British snipe
does, although the sound produced was louder and somewhat
different in character, more like grinding or whetting, occasionally
one heard the chuck-chucking sound down among the herbage in
the marsh, and very soon one of the performing birds would swoop
down and drop on to the ground at the very spot. But whether the
call of the female was in response to a wooer or from a bird already
paired to its mate I never discovered. Seebohm[9] has nothing about
this chucking cry or call, nor has Shaw in his book on the snipe in
the Fur and Feather series.[10] I doubt if any of the books will
enlighten you about it.

I have never had an opportunity of visiting the Dartford
Warbler's haunt you told me of, but am glad to hear the birds still
exist. Most of my rambles of late have been in West Cornwall.[11]
One small colony of the bird survives there about half way between
Penzance and the Land's End.

The place on the Lymington River near Boldre where I
stayed is –

Roydon House,
Boldre,
Lymington.

They take in visitors, and if you go there to stay you will find the
people very kind. Their name is Hooker. But I believe they get a
good many visitors there now so that you cannot rely on getting
accommodation. The best plan is to write to Mrs Hooker some
time before you go. It is a long time since I have been there and it
may not be quite so charmingly wild as when I described it in
Hampshire Days.[12]

5

(8 March [1909] from 40 St Lukes Road, W.)

The Peruvian bird your friend describes is a stone curlew and resembles our bird very much except in its broad black eye-stripe. It is the –
Oedicnemus superciliaris
and is confined to Peru, or at all events to that part of the South American continent. Of course I have never seen it as it does not range to the Atlantic side. The natives call it Juancito – Little Jack, and all we have about its habits is a note by the bird collector Stolzmann, quoted by L. Jaczanowski, in his third volume (*Ornithologie du Peru*) – the only work I know on Peruvian birds. Stolzmann says just what your friend has written about the bird and the way the natives have of swathing its legs in red flannel (goodness knows why!) and tying little bells to them.

I did not know you had written about our stone curlew in *Country Life*. I do not often see it. I daresay you have read Edmund Selous' account of his observations of the bird in *Bird Watching*.[13] I think the best account I have read of the bird – at all events the best written, is by Trevor-Battye in a little book of his called *Prose Idylls*.[14] Trevor-Battye was a good observer and a charming writer but he is too lazy or too well off to do much.

6

(19 August [1909] from Heytesbury, Wiltshire[15])

I know the road and the spot you describe as a breeding place of the curlews very well. When I was staying in May and June at Hindon on the other side of the Great Ridge Wood I used to come out at that point and ramble about the downs where the road comes down to Sherrington. It was not far from the wood and quite close to the road or track that I found a nest with a single egg in it.

It looked very freshly laid and the birds were near, so I left it a good many days but when I returned there was no egg and no bird about. On the other side of the ridge another pair laid two eggs quite close to the wood but the confounded keeper who lives at that point (at Penning House) took the eggs.

I have been staying at Codford but did not hear about the peregrine. The fact is, this summer I have thought little about birds and have not been watching for them. But one thing I am convinced of and that is there are no kingfishers in the Wylye. Whether the anglers are to blame for it or not I can't say.

Another thing: you can hear the cirl bunting in every one of the twenty or twenty-five villages and hamlets between Warminster and Salisbury. Goldfinches too are pretty common all along the valley. But on the whole Wiltshire is rather poor in birds, I fancy.

———————————

7

(9 July 1910 from 40 St Lukes Road, W.)

Thanks for your letter telling me about the Wylye kingfishers and the stone curlews.

I haven't been to that part this season – or not since last March – but was in Dorset and Somerset last month. I wanted to find the woodlark but did not succeed and the only people I found at Blandford, Wimborne and at Wells and Glastonbury and some other places who know about the birds told me there is no woodlark in that part of the country. I was at Bradbury Rings to enquire about the ravens that used to build there. A few years ago Mr Bosworth Smith wrote that they had returned to this ancient haunt, but it was not true, the people of the place told me.

I had a better time in May in the Peak District and was lucky enough to find a cottage to stay in up on Axe Edge, near Buxton. There were ring and water ouzels,[16] sandpipers, curlew and golden plover breeding. The species I went chiefly to see was the ring ouzel, as I had never had an opportunity of watching and listening

to it properly in its breeding season. The bird was quite common on the hill where I stayed – one pair had their nest within a few minutes' walk of the cottage and I got to know the bird intimately during my stay.

Unfortunately this has been another wet cold season for the birds – and their watchers, and upon the Peak the weather is always worse than anywhere else. The saying is that if there is any bad weather in England it will be there.

Have you been to the Zoological Gardens to see the Cock of the Rock?[17] I enclose a couple of tickets in case you want to go on a Sunday.[18] My visits are generally on a Saturday afternoon when the band plays on the lawn. It is a pleasant resting place – but the weather is against us this season.

8

(20 February 1911 from 40 St Lukes Road, W.)

Your letters always interest me greatly so please don't apologise for them. For the last two or three days, oddly enough, it has been in my mind to write to you. A long time ago you told me about finding a colony of Dartford warblers at a spot somewhere on the border of Hants and Wilts – Grateley way; and I now find I have mislaid the reference and would like you to tell me the exact locality again. I want, if I have the opportunity when in the country this Spring to look up some of the colonies of this warbler.

The blackbird story is very interesting – I suppose it is true and that your friend actually witnessed what he relates himself and has woven the incident into his story. I wonder if he can give a more exact description of the bird? It happens that there are at least *five* species of blackbird (*Merula*) in Peru and without knowing the size, colour and other points it would be hard to say what the species is. As to the sex, his bird was undoubtedly a male as in the thrushes the female as a rule does not sing. Furthermore the female in most species differs in colour, being much lighter than the male – brown in most species. Male birds often do 'mother' an orphaned fledgeling.

A brief description of the five species known to inhabit Peru might enable your friend to identify the species:

1. Peruvian giant blackbird – *Merula giantodes*. More than a third larger than the English blackbird. Dusky black – legs as well as beak, and eyelids orange yellow. A very sweet singer – the natives say it has seven songs.
2. Giant ouzel – these English names are only book-names. *M. gigas*. Resembles the first in colouring, nothing about its song reported.
3. D'Orbigney's ouzel. *M. fuscata*. Like our blackbird in size. Dull sooty brownish black. Sings or whistles like our bird – some say sweeter. Ranges into Argentina.
4. White-eyed ouzel. *M. leucops*. Smaller than our blackbird. Very black colour. Has a varied but not very musical song – sings on the high tree tops.
5. Peruvian black ouzel. *M. serrana*. A little less in size than our bird. Found in forests, but nothing of its song known.

All these blackbirds have yellow legs as well as beak. They have various Indian names, but the Spanish call them *Mirlo* – the European name.

I wonder if your friend's book is published? I wish he could tell us just what the song of his bird was like.

9

(25 March [1911] from 40 St Lukes Road, W.)

Thanks for telling me about the blackbird. If I had heard that peculiar note of distress in them I must have forgotten it. It is one of our very commonest birds yet I suppose there are things to be learnt about it still. For instance, it is often stated that it breaks snail-shells by striking them against a stone as thrushes do, yet I have never detected them in the act, but I have seen them watch and follow a thrush and when he has broken the shell down the blackbird has dropped upon him and deprived him of the snail. The thrush meekly drops his snail just as a small dog drops a bone when a big dog comes on the scene and orders him to do so and tells him with a growl it will be bad for him if he doesn't.

I must go back to the blackbird when I am out of London again – a succession of colds and the ungenial weather have prevented me from getting away so far.

(P.S.) I don't think the proposed changes in St James Park will be carried out.

10

(20 June [1912] from 40 St Lukes Road, W.)

Alas, dear Mr Harding, there is little help in me now and that 'powerful pen' you mention has now about as much virtue as may be found in a straw blown about in the street. Ill-health, my own and my wife's, has kept me a close prisoner in London for the last *ten months*. In all that time I have not been so far as Richmond nor Kew. An eternity practically. I doubt if such a place as Wimbledon Common exists: it is nothing but a memory – an old tradition. How could I write of such things! You say you are collecting money in a small way: can small contributions count for anything at all in such a matter? I can send a guinea and that's all I could do at present – and as for the future, I doubt if there will be one.

I was much interested in your 'Saturday'[19] article. I used to spend a good deal of time in the Gardens, the Queen's Cottage grounds especially before the path was made for the public.[20] The Director (Thiselton-Dyer)[21] wanted me to contribute a paper on the birds to a volume of the Kew Bulletin on the Flora and Fauna of the Gardens. It was published in 1906. I used often to hear the lesser spotted woodpecker there, but did not admit the great spotted in the lists. If you would like to see the Bulletin I will send it to you.[22]

The *Saturday Reveiew* has some papers I wrote about my

birding rambles fourteen months ago, but the Editor often keeps things a long time.[23]

I I

(26 July 1912 from 15 Grosvenor Road, Lowestoft, Suffolk)

I had your letter this morning at Norwich and wondered at your thinking the words I used in the account of the Dartford warbler flattering. I fancy it is the very truth that you do have a secret delight and happiness in your communings with nature.[24] It was my forgetfulness not to have written and told you I had found the birds at that spot you directed me to. It was on Hartford Bridge Flats and the village I did *not* stay at was Sandhurst. I stayed at Yateley on the border of the common. I found the Dartford in three separate places, but the spot where they were abundant was near the main road across the flats on the right hand join from Blackwater and about the middle of the flats, where the furze grows very luxuriantly.

Mr Hodge, the Editor of the 'Saturday' told me he would print *four* articles; if he had not made that condition or restriction I would have been able to describe the song of the marsh warbler, which I came upon further west. I suppose that will have to remain now until I can print a collection of bird papers in volume form.[25]

Unfortunately this has been a black year for me owing to illness, my wife's and my own. She is pretty well again, altho' weak, and I am not up to much and it is too late to find anything fresh now. I spent a day at Thetford hunting for the woodlark, hoping to hear it sing even at the end of July. I had heard that a few pairs still breed in some fields near Croxton, about two miles from Thetford, in the direction of Norwich, but I didn't succeed in finding them. Skylarks I saw and heard in the fields, but no woodlarks. There is reason to fear that these few pairs have been or will be exterminated by the collectors, as all that portion of Norfolk is their happiest hunting ground, including the Elvedon estate.

I shall stay a few days here and then probably go inland some-where either in Norfolk or Suffolk for two or three weeks longer before returning to London.

I 2

(9 November 1912 from 40 St Lukes Road, W.)

I'm sorry I can't help you: my memory for these things is not over-good and probably I never saw the sentence. It has rather a 17th-century sound and might be in Walton. I can't even remem-ber the name of any other Jacobean or Caroline who said anything in praise of birds – in prose, I mean. With the poets of that period I have a better acquaintance as I have a taste for their peculiar view.

I am just back from Wells-next-the-sea where I always go if possible in October to see the wild geese. The Wells people say they never had a greater number than this year. There must have been over four thousand in a vast flock I saw a few evenings ago on the return of the birds from feeding on the inland pasture-lands to their roosting-places on the sands. It was a grand spectacle! Hooded crows and fieldfares were coming in very large numbers too.

Before going to Wells I spent some weeks in South Devon, mostly at Sidmouth and I met there a native wild naturalist, a gardener named Ernest Salley, who knows a good deal about local bird life and is a perfect enthusiast. On the Sidmouth cliffs I saw two pairs of ravens on several occasions. Both pairs breed on the cliffs, one near Bere, the other pair between Sidmouth and Budleigh.

I hope you had a good holiday in some bird-haunted place.

13

(*29 December 1912 from 40 St Lukes Road, W.*)

Thanks for the little owl card – it is a good likeness of the bird which I seldom see. I do not know if you go often to the zoo but will send you a few tickets.

I saw your letter in the *Field* and wonder if the yellow wagtail still breeds in Richmond Park. It is so long since I have rambled there in the summer time I do not know whether the bird is ever seen there or not now. This wagtail is one of our songsters the song of which I do not know, and very few of our ornithologists do know it, I think. It is said by one who has heard it that it resembles the song of the pied wagtail and that the bird utters it while fluttering in the air. The pied bird sings both on the ground and in the air but the song is louder and finer when the bird mounts up a few yards to sing. In Spring it sometimes utters a low warble which goes on for a long time without a break. But the strange thing about all wagtails is that they sing so seldom. One observer who has heard the yellow wagtail says that it may pass many days without attempting to sing.

I have just finished a book of Adventures among Birds, as I call it, in which I have included most of the bird articles I have written during the last two or three years, with a good deal of added matter. Hutchinson has taken it and will bring it out in Spring, I suppose.[26]

Just now I am thinking of going to Cornwall for a while as I am in poor health which sets me longing for the pure fresh air and granite cliffs and blue seas of the Land's End country.

With all good wishes for 1913.

14

(26 January 1913 from 40 St Lukes Road, W.)

Your letter was received two or three weeks ago and was not
answered at once as my wife was very ill again and I let everything
else go by the board. She is just recovering now from a very
serious attack of bronchitis. Her illness prevented my going away
to Cornwall at the beginning of this month. I may get away in
February if she goes on all right now.

The passage I quoted in *Wild Wings* was from Thomson's
Seasons: –

'What is this mighty breath, ye sages say,
That in a powerful language, felt not heard,
Instructs the fowls of Heaven?'[27]

It is in 'Spring' and refers to the pairing passion in birds; but in
the 'Autumn' there are some notable passages about migration,
especially one describing the phenomenon in the Western Islands:–

'where the Atlantic surge
Boils round the naked melancholy isles.'

'There is no doubt' say the critics, 'that Thomson wrote a vicious
style'. Well, I love his style chiefly on account of what they are
pleased to call its viciousness. It is what we call in Spanish a
retumbanté style[28] and is I suppose too sounding and Miltonic to
suit the modern taste.

Are you a collector of passages about birds? There are several
bird poem anthologies but they are all unsatisfactory. I want to do
one myself on different lines but doubt if I shall ever have the time
to make the collection and write the comments. The usual plan is
just to shovel up a lot of stuff, good, bad and indifferent, until the
book is full; and no comments at all.

There is a good deal about play in birds in the book I have
written – I could have written much more if there had been space.[29]
Your story of the peacock in St James' Park reminded me of an
incident at the zoo of two vultures playing with a wing feather
which one dropped from its wing. It was an amusing exhibition but
it saddened one at the same time to see these poor wretched
prisoners for life trying to get a little happiness out of the fallen
feather.

As you have been reading the *Naturalist in La Plata*[30] I

33

should like to know if you have come across *Idle Days in Patagonia*?[31] Dent is thinking of getting out a cheap edition of that book, but I have a number of copies of the first edition and it would please me very much to give you a copy if you have not got one already. Please let me know if I may send it.

(P.S.) About the cuckoo heard in December. I heard a wryneck calling in February a few years ago but could not see the bird. I believe now it must have been a starling – a perfect mimic!

----

1 5

(19 May 1913 from 40 St Lukes Road, W.)

I envy you the days at Codford and all other green places where you have been – I haven't stirred from London yet, and if I do get out of town it will only be to take my wife somewhere and be with her. So there will be no birds for me *this* season – excepting the ruffian sparrows and a pair of wood pigeons who coo to me at four every morning and feed from a bird-tray at my window.

My new book will be issued tomorrow but I got some copies at the publishers today and shall have much pleasure in sending one for your acceptance.[32] Of course you have read a good deal of the matter contained in the volume in magazines, but there is much you haven't seen and one chapter about the marsh warbler. I am sorry the publisher has seen fit to put in a rather ugly photograph of me as a frontispiece. The book is his and he can do as he likes about such things. I should have preferred the book without such a questionable ornament.

16

Thanks for your letter and the offer of tickets for a theatre. They are very acceptable at most times, but at present I find it impossible to go owing to my wife's condition. It is odd you suggested *Typhoon*. A few days ago I called to see a lady friend who had just started that short correspondence in the Mail about the play and found Lawrence Irving and his wife there.[33] I had to confess I had not seen the play and added that I would try to get to the theatre on the Saturday. He generously sent me a box for that day, and after all I couldn't go! And that's as near being at a play as I have got these four months. Perhaps when you are performing yourself next time you will send me a seat.

I don't know that Irving cares anything about natural history, but I know he detests vivisection which means that he is a lover of animals, so that we have one feeling in common. Miss Lind-af-Hageby[34] is our chief heroine just now.

About the nightingales at Wimbledon, I had a letter three or four days ago from a friend who is devoted to birds tho' his years are spent in a City Bank, telling me of *four* nightingales on the Common. And you also make them four!

It is good news that so great a bird as the great spotted woodpecker has taken possession of one of our nesting boxes.[35]

That pretending to be a young bird by the female when fed by her mate is not uncommon – I have observed it in a number of species, but never in any pigeon. They are all amorous birds but their exceeding greediness gets the better of their love. Our lovely wood pigeon is a flagrant example. *My* bird here performs his love flights over the chimney-pots in fine style but when he comes to feed on corn on the bird-tray at the window he devours all or all he can stuff down while his mate stands humbly by waiting till he has finished before daring to touch a grain.

———————————

17

(15 June [1913] from 3 West View, Pelham Road, Seaford)

Many thanks for your offer of tickets for *Panthea* but at present we are out of London. We have been here for a fortnight with not much benefit so far, but are going to try another week before giving Seaford up as an unsuitable place for my wife's illness.

About the marsh warblers, you will have to go to Gloucester to find the particular colony I referred to. One part of it – the nearest – is very near the city. It is up the Severn, and instead of taking the road, you walk out past the Cathedral and find a footpath over the fields and so make a short cut to an old hedge sheltering an osier bed – the first one you come to, and there you would find the birds. They will just be nesting now.

I'm sorry the Richmond Park nesting boxes have been thrown down. I often wonder if a love – a protecting love – of birds will ever get instilled into the people generally!

Here I find one curious thing, where buildings, golf-links, etc have driven out the birds there used to be. A few wheatears have refused to quit, and two pairs have nested in some chalk emptied into a depression in one of the building-lots not yet sold. I look right down from my window at the nesting spot and the birds flitting about. The nesting holes are only a few yards back from the Parade and less than a stone's throw from a shelter. All day long people are going and coming or sitting close to them, and they go on with their business just the same. The young have just come off – one bird in one case and three in the other. One would hardly expect to find wheatears breeding, and getting their young off, in a town!

Should I be back in London before *Panthea* is withdrawn, I will manage somehow to see it. I did not think from the notices that it was going to be a success.

————————

18

(*Sunday Evening* [*July or August 1913*] *from Thistle Grove, Furze Platt, Maidenhead.*)

We have settled here for the present, just to see how it will suit my wife's case: she continues about the same.

I am glad you succeeded in finding the marsh warblers and only wish you could have spent some days with them. The five or six days I spent listening to them seemed to me only too short a time. I fancy they must have been driven from the osier bed where I found them as it was that very bed with a high bank and tall hedge row elms at the side where I found so many pairs in full song and breeding.

About the swifts. I think it is known now that the male often absents himself at night although it has not been proved that he spends the whole night in flying about at a great height. An account of the observations of a country clergyman was given in a Natural History publication two or three years ago. Several pairs of swifts bred in a large loft to which the clergyman could gain access through a trapdoor at night. On many nights the females alone were on the nest. He would pick them up and hold them in his hand and then replace them on their nests, the birds taking the handling very quietly. Then on other nights he would find all the males roosting with their mates on the nests. These were generally cool evenings. On still other evenings a few males would be present, others absent. I have often watched swifts rise up during the breeding season at 9.0 to 9.30 of an evening and finally disappear at a great height and have watched in vain for their return. However, the question is not likely to be settled for a long time yet.

19

(23 December 1913 from 40 St Lukes Road, W.)

Thank you for your kind greeting and good wishes for the season. We are in just about the same condition as when I wrote last: I see no prospect of any change at present in my wife's health, and I of course suffer through being forced to remain in town for so many months at a stretch.

I hope the play you appeared in at the Shaftesbury will be put on somewhere, as judging from the notice I saw in the *Observer* it must be good and well played.

I managed to get to the Queen's Theatre to see you in the play there and got very good seats in the circle, front row. I enjoyed it very much and I think your part was the best in the piece and charmingly acted. After reading John Palmer's article about it I expected as much. He also gave great praise to Miss Jerrold, but I don't think she was quite flawless: yours was perfect.[36]

With good wishes for the New Year.

(P.S.) It was to the Saturday matinée I went at the Queen's – three weeks ago – as I could not get out for an evening.

20

(31 March [1914] from 40 St Lukes Road, W.)

Thanks for your letter and for calling to see me the other day. I wish I had been a little better as we might then have had our first meeting.

If they say I am mending – the two doctors who have been attending me and my Scottish servant woman, or 'body', who gave you the information – it is perhaps all right. But I am rather sceptical about any considerable progress healthwards as I think this attack has cut in too deeply.[37] At all events the aforesaid two doctors are calling in a third to confer with them over me one day this week. Meanwhile I'm just able now to get up a little.

I'm glad you saw that owl as I'm always anxious about him.

---

2 1

(*22 April [1914] from The Cottage, Park Road, Worthing*)

I was sorry the other day to miss you when you kindly called to enquire and I was out for my constitutional – or daily crawl. I am gradually mending but can't walk but short distances yet without great fatigue. If I succeed in finding a comfortable home for my wife here in some private house I shall try to go on to Cornwall where I would just now most like to be.

Yesterday I disturbed a turtle dove in a baytree a few yards from the front door here, and it only flew reluctantly a few yards away and settled again. It struck me that it had just arrived from over the Channel and was too exhausted to be wild. I asked my landlady if she had a tame turtle dove about the place and she replied that she didn't know what a turtle dove was. She kept no birds but fowls. Still the place is pretty full of birds and the starlings nesting on the house come right to the door for bread.

I am sending you a few Zoo tickets I have in my pocket book which you may find a use for.

---

2 2

(*10 June [1914] from 40 St Lukes Road, W.*)

I return the three tickets with three more, all signed this time. I found I had sent others to a friend also unsigned, but she

39

happened to be a female, a suffragist too though a non-militant, and so boldly put my name to the cards and found it all right.

I was sorry your little Lamb had so brief an existence: I was not well enough to go and see it when it was on. I hope you will have something more lasting next time.

That faculty of mimicry in our song birds is very queer. One goes on listening to some common songster for years without hearing any variations in its song, then all at once you come on one like your blackcap – a perfect original – or rather mocker: a sort of bird genius. I have unhappily been out of it this season, and now it is pretty well over.

I am still suffering from a weak heart. My wife is rather better at Worthing than she was here, as she stays out of doors a good deal down there. I go to her for the week-ends. But there has been no visit to Cornwall.

23

(21 March [1915] from 40 St Lukes Road, W.)

If you will allow it – but I don't 'Mister' any of my friends – why should I make an exception? And I don't suppose you like 'Mister'-ing yours.[38]

If I had got your letter first post instead of the last one (9.30) you could have had the tickets for today – a nice Spring day too, just right for the Zoo.

By chance I am here just now for a short time: for the last year I've mostly been away, part of the time at Worthing with my wife and partly at Ascot at a friend's house.[39] My wife is about the same – just strong enough to take a short walk with her companion, but she makes no progress to better health. Nor can I say much for my own, else I should have gone further afield before now. However, I hope to get to Cornwall (Land's End and that part) early in April when the gorse is at its best. A friend will motor me there[40] and that will give me a better sight of the long road than one has in a railway carriage.

I'm glad you are doing something for the country at present.[41] There is no satisfaction for anyone now in any other kind of work. Even my poor wife has occupied herself since September last in knitting garments for the men in the trenches, and to be able to do that much has given her a kind of happiness. But almost every list contains names of bright young lives that have been given for the Cause – lives of those we knew or sons of friends. It is a tremendous war – but one dreams and hopes – a regenerating war for England and perhaps for all Europe.[42]

24

(24 June 1915 from Grey Friars, Ascot)

Thanks for yours and for sending me your French friend's letter to read. It is most interesting and what he says in appreciation of the English in the war is a pleasure to read. I showed the letter to the Ranee of Sarawak with whom I am staying here and she was so delighted with it she took down the address so as to send him one or two of Jefferies' books – I think she will send him *The Story of my Heart* which is a revelation to those who have never read Jefferies.[43] His word anent my books are very gratifying.

I didn't get much benefit from my visit to Cornwall as I couldn't get fit for walking, but all the same I got about a good deal in the car during the five weeks I had at Lelant, visiting all my old haunts as far as I could and seeing old friends. On our way back we tried the Tavistock route but found the hills too steep for the rather weak car and at some hills had to get out and walk. During one of these ascents I discovered a most lovely wild flower I had never seen before – the Bastard Balm, the *Melisse des Bois* of the French, a flower of the same tribe as the dead nettle but much larger – cream white, with a purple lip. Finally we had to abandon that route and go twenty miles or so round to the other one which goes by Okehampton.

I am glad you can still get out to the parks and see birds. In the pine woods not many yards from the house here there are a lot

43

of jays, magpies and one or two pairs of hawks breeding. Foxes and hedgehogs also abound and my only complaint is that there are no adders and snakes to add to the variety. I was near Hartford Bridge Flat a few days ago, but in the car and to look for birds was impossible. I hope you'll go and find the Dartford still there.

25

(11 July [1915] from Grey Friars, Ascot.)

Thanks for telling me about the woodlark: I went over yesterday but could not see the dead pine tree you described so went to the lodge to enquire, and the woman told me they had just cut it down for firewood! However, I found the bird singing on another tree close by and listened to him for some time. But he would not sing freely and there was much to disturb him; four or five boys from the lodge with a goat or kid, and men cutting trees just inside the wood. If I could have gone in the late evening or at 5.0 o'clock in the morning it would have been better I dare say; but it would not be possible for me to get the car here at such hours. And I cannot cycle now with my bad heart.

The last woodlark I heard before this bird was on that immense heath lying between Fordingbridge and Brockenhurst. I was cycling over it towards evening after a rainy day and found the bird using a small tree at the roadside and singing continually and thought it the sweetest bird song I had ever heard. Since then I have visited many places in search of the bird without success. It is I fear becoming very rare now.

The best thing we have here just now is a brood of four young sparrowhawks in a pine tree quite near the house. It is a tall tree but with little foliage and standing on a hillock close by one can look at the nest with the binocular and see all four young birds quite plainly and watch their doings. Yesterday two of the young looking like owls sat side by side in the middle of the nest apparently surveying the scene and elbowing one another: a third stood up on the rim of the nest shaking his wings as if wishing to fly, and

44

the fourth had dragged a small bird to the opposite side and was tearing at it. Sometimes they drop a bird, and it looks as if it had been plucked and prepared for cooking at a poulterer's shop, so well do the old birds clean it of feathers. They also take off the head, which I fancy they swallow themselves.

Yesterday we had a hedgehog in the strawberry bed tangled in the net. He was liberated, but about 10.0 o'clock in the evening the same little beast probably turned up at the open door of the kitchen. The cook put some bread down which the little pig ate and then walked off. They are strangely confiding little beasts and I believe if you catch one and keep it a day or two in confinement it will become perfectly tame and stay about the house.

By-the-by, the old hawks here are excessively shy and slip away and vanish when we go near the tree.

26

(24 April [1918] from 23 North Parade, Penzance.[44]*)*

I am delighted to have a letter from you after so long. I have been away from London for about five months now, to escape the winter, but we've had it cold enough this Spring. As to the birds, they are rare in Penzance and about this part of the country. But a few days ago going from here by train to Lelant – a village seven miles away, after passing Marazion – a village near Penzance, the train runs through a marshy ground with patches of reeds – dead and yellow now – and out of a patch as the train ran past flapped a big yellow bird, and after going twenty yards dropped down again and stood with neck stretched up: – a bittern! The first one I've ever caught sight of in a wild state! But a good many have been shot this winter in different parts of the country.[45]

I don't remember just where Davidson describes the oboe voice of the blackbird. I may be able to find it when I get back to my books. Poor D. met his end here when in despair he drowned himself in the Bay.[46]

I fancy the larger illustrated edition of *A Shepherd's Life*[47] is out of print now, and that it can only be got in Methuen's Shilling Editions. Well, I had to cut it down for those small cheap editions and it is perhaps that one you have read. Still, there's a good deal about dogs in it (and about the Shepherd's own people too). I spent more time in getting all the facts in the history of that family than in any other work I have ever done. The poor old Shepherd is dead now, but he had a tremendous time of joyful excitement when he had the book sent to him by a gentleman living in that part of the country who had identified the character.[48]

I daresay I shall be going up to the region called in Cornwall 'Up Along' before many days. I haven't seen my wife since the beginning of December and must go to Worthing to see her, then to London; but I intend spending a few days at Exeter, as it is one of my favourite towns, and I like to haunt the Cathedral. Then too the apple is beginning to blossom and I must have a little time among the apple-orchards near Exeter.[49]

(P.S.) I saw some time ago that your uncle at Codford had left a big fortune and sincerely hope you were benefited to some extent.

27

(9 July [1918] from Ascot Wood Cottage, Ascot)

Your letter comes to me here. I fled from influenza in London as it broke out in the house – two of the inmates had it there, one being my housekeeper – and now it has burst on us here! I am staying here with my old friend the Ranee of Sarawak who considers herself the most perfectly healthy woman in England, and now at noon today she was suddenly bowled over and has a temperature of 103! Where I'm to go I don't know, unless it be back to London and then perhaps to Worthing where my wife is: only she says there's no accommodation now in all the place. Must consider the position tonight.[50]

Do you know, I don't think there's anything strange or very

uncommon in all you tell me about that nervous condition you have been in. I have myself known those fantastic fears and tremors, and have been frightened at a mole – a less formidable creature than a stoat. By the by it is quite true that stoats have followed and attacked human beings. Also a family of weasels have been known to do such a thing. But the thought and fear of such a thing is a sign of nerves, of course – a sign that you have been going down in your long work in town and want more red blood, which you can only get by changing your way of life or the time you give each day to work, unless you can take a good long holiday which would be the best thing. What a pity you couldn't stay on in Exmoor for two or three months! Another friend on holiday has lately written to me twice from Simonsbath. He too went away very much run down and in a nervous state and is now getting all right. And he, too, Morley Roberts,[51] had been working too much and keeping too long at it without a break.

I'm sorry I haven't been able to go any further than Surrey and Sussex this Summer, and have seen and heard little. I heard some birds, including the nightingale, at Pepperharrow,[52] and that neighbourhood, but I would have given all the bird songs there for the ring ouzel's strain.

About the redstarts on Exmoor and in Richmond Park, my idea is that all the songbirds near London, as well as in it, have degenerated as singers. I think there's something in the conditions that tell against them. However, I may be wrong, but the redstart does certainly sing a very inferior song in the parks near London – Richmond and Woolwich and Blackheath is where I have heard him chiefly.

I think those strange cries you heard at night may have proceeded from the barn owl. If you have never heard their cries when the old birds turn upon and try to hunt their young or other invading individuals out of their territory you can't imagine the weird and extraordinary sounds they emit. It is however, a rare thing to hear them – at their best.

To go back: your old Niagra experience is similar to one I had at the Valley of the Rocks near Lynton, when going by that very narrow footpath along the side of a slope, where you look down to the sea some hundreds of feet below you, and know that if your foot slipped you would roll right down over the smooth slope. It affected me so that I had to sit down and keep my eyes away from the slope for some time before I ventured to proceed.

I am just correcting the last proofs of a book of early memories
– a sort of history of my boyhood, which Dent will publish about
September.[53]

28

(27 July [1918] from 40 St Lukes Road, W.11.)

I'm sorry I can't find the poem with the blackbird passage in
Davidson: I can in fact find only one of his books on my shelves –
one of the Testaments[54] – and fancy I lent the others to some
friend and forgot to make a note of it. But it may have been to a
friend who went to the war but will return no more.

Just now I have been turning out a mass of old letters to look
them over before destroying most of them and came on one in
which T. E. Brown's[55] lines on the blackbird are quoted: probably
you know them, but I will send you the letter as I think it will
amuse you. To come across a woman who has read Drayton's
Polyolbion[56] *three* times is too delicious. But she writes delight-
fully, only I can't agree that there is anything Blackbirdy in
Alfred Noyes.[57] Please return the two letters some day: they are
worth keeping.

I wonder if you too flirt with the notion of a bird Anthology!
Well it won't clash with mine (which will never materialize) as
I'm going on a system of my own.

29

([58]September [1918] from 40 St Lukes Road, W.11.)

I haven't seen the last *Field*: I've been nursing a cold for
some days and have been out very little, so have not looked at the

50

weeklies. But I fancy the Raven story is almost too absurd to notice, and I wonder Harting[59] could put it in without any enquiry as to its truth. No doubt the birds are the common crows which roam all over London and haunt any open space where they can pick up a bone or a crust. There is always a pair at Kensington Gardens and others at Kenwood and at other places. One pair visits my street on most days – they are going to or from Hyde Park, I think, and are probably the same birds that visit the Paddington Recreation Ground.

30

(12 March 1920 from 23 North Parade, Penzance)

Your letter has been sent on to me here where I have been in my usual winter quarters since early in November with no desire to leave them till about the end of May.

It was a surprise to me to find you are still occupied with Red Cross work. I had imagined you had finished with it after the war, and as I had not seen your return to the stage I formed the idea that you had gone to nature and have been envying your good fortune. For I am doomed to an indoor life for the rest of my time, as my heart is weak and a little exercise soon exhausts me so I can go no rambles. I still write and have books on the stocks, but writing books is not living – not the life I want. I have more material than I shall ever use up and so must be satisfied with this re-living in the past and get what happiness I can out of it.

I had got about half a book written when I came here,[60] but have been unwell most of the time, and then started on a new thing – a story[61] – so the Nature subject has not been restarted yet.

You ask if my books sell well: I have no interest in the books written for some years past as I sell the copyrights out and out: but I'm pretty sure they do sell as three or four publishers give me eight or nine times more than I should have ventured to ask for a book a few years ago. In America they are now having a great vogue and I receive a perpetual stream of letters from readers over there from all over the country, from the Atlantic States to California, and from Florida and Louisiana to Seattle, Vancouver, etc. And they are many of them extremely interesting about the curious things observed in animal habits. Those of my books most read in America are *Far Away and Long Ago*,[62] *Green Mansions*[63] and *The Book of a Naturalist*[64] – my last work. The romance *Green Mansions*, after having been published twenty years only began to sell there about four years ago and has gone into about ten editions in that time. It had never been copyrighted in America, but the publisher gives me a royalty all the same. In England the copyrights of these old romances still belong to me, and they still have a sale. The sales, the publishers tell me, are improving.

You were very lucky in hearing all those warblers – which I shall never hear. But on the other hand I've heard the marsh warbler which has I think, the best song of all the warblers. I used to long to be able to go to Holland or Belgium to hear the golden oriole and the cry of the great black woodpecker, also the *hoop-hoop* of the hoopoe. Once only have I heard the golden oriole in England, in one of its two breeding-places where it still comes in Spring, or did a few years ago.

The lines on the goldfinch I don't know: why not send them to the *Observer* and ask for the author? They are putting such requests and answers in every week now in the correspondence columns.

I can always give you Zoo tickets when you want any.

Here we have had no winter weather this season, and for a month past it has been full spring.

---

3 1

([65]*March [1920] from 23 North Parade, Penzance*)

I enclose half a dozen tickets for the Zoo. I don't know who our Secretary is, now Chalmers Mitchell[66] is himself caged in Africa where so many of his big captives come from.

I see your goldfinch query is in Sunday's *Observer*, so shall look excitedly at the paper next Sunday.

Among my letters this morning from readers of my last two books, there's one from a man who tells me that the name of the wagtail in Arabic means the 'Father of Salutation'. I wish I had known that before. It is lovely, I think – the wagtail's characteristic expression from the Arabian point of view.

I hope you will enjoy Shropshire.

---

3 2

(3 July 1920 from 40 St Lukes Road, W.11)

I can't tell you. Long Ditton is sacred to no one I can recall.[67] 'The blackbirds with their oboe voices' sounds well, mainly I daresay because oboe has been used by no one in this connection, whereas we are always comparing the bird's voice to a flute. But the true word *is* the flute: of all our musical instruments it comes nearest to the blackbird, just as a very pure and tender contralto is the nearest to it in human singing. The best sounds of the oboe are very like flute sounds, but in its higher tones there is a catty quality which to my taste at all events detracts from its charm. The blackbird has many bad sounds – gurgling, squealing, squeaking sounds, which rival those of a thrush trying to be original or, shall we say, indulging in a songbird's *vers libre*? But neither thrush or blackbird are ever catty; and that's where they differ from their first cousins, the mocking-birds.

One is sad to think of poor John Davidson's fate.[68] Good as he was, he never succeeded in getting properly recognised. And I believe he was poor and found his life very hard, then came his miserable end at Penzance where he threw himself into the sea. When his last poems were appearing – the *Testaments* – some people thought he had gone a little off his head. Certainly he took himself as a poet-prophet with tremendous seriousness in those painful poems. But they had great power. He was once on the staff of the *Speaker* – mainly reviewing books – and I remember he wrote a (to me) delightful review of my old book *Birds in a Village*.[69]

33

(29 March 1921 from 23 North Parade, Penzance)

Thank you, my dear Harding, for your sympathy. I have unfortunately been ill for a long time past, and as my doctor told me it would be death to me to attempt to travel to Worthing I could not attend at the interment of my wife.[70]

34

(20 May 1921 from 23 North Parade, Penzance)

Pardon delay in answering your letter and thanking you for the magazine. I have not read it yet as I have not had the time to look at anything except a book or two bearing on the question of animal's instinct. I am just now trying to do a chapter or two on migration and it is a long and difficult subject, and until I get over it I can't proceed with the book I began more than a year ago.[71] I have really not touched it since I came here until the last week or two, as I am feeling a little better just now.

I daresay the swift and sand-swallow[72] you saw were resting on their journey to the North. Our swifts arrived on April 29 – just the usual number and they spend half the day darting up and down before my windows for they breed on this terrace. But not a swallow nor a martin. I have been taking a few motor rides this week and last week and so far have only seen one swallow a few miles from Penzance. What a calamity if that bird so universal a favourite and so associated with the home feeling in all the country should be dying out entirely!

The woodpeckers are safer in London than they would be in any wood or forest in the country where keepers shoot them to give a pretty bird to some friend or to their children.

A friend of mine at the Chart in Kent has seen three golden orioles in the woods there – and heard them.

I shall go up to London next week I think.

35

(1 January 1922 from 23 North Parade, Penzance)

Thanks for the letter and good wishes. My health is pretty much in the same state as last year at this time and the year before, and I came here as usual at the end of November to escape the deadly London winter atmosphere. Not before the late November fogs had almost suffocated me. Here, although wet almost all the time one can breathe, and it is very mild. Also we have some glimpses of sunshine and I take some runs in a car to the places about these parts where I have friends to visit.

I am glad you consented to go on the R.S.P.B. Council and hope when I return – if I ever do – in May I shall be able to go to the Council Meetings and that we may meet there.[73]

Here I see little bird life and don't know a single being in this town or in any town or village in this west end of Cornwall that takes any interest in this subject. Here there is a solicitor – Harvey by name – who boasts that he has the best collection of ornithological works in Cornwall. So he has, but it is books, books, books with him rather than the living bird. And books are a weariness to a man accustomed to live with living things. All I can do now is just to go on working with my unused notes, and there is more material than I shall ever be able to use up, as I go very slowly now.

With all good wishes for the New Year.

36

(5 February 1922 from 23 North Parade, Penzance[74])

I saw the paragraph in the *Times* and had already heard you had been appointed on the Committee.[75] You are the very man for it, and need no hints from me as you are more familiar with the Royal Parks and their bird life than any man in London. All can see that from your *Field* and *Nineteenth Century* writings. I am glad that Lord Crawford is the head of it as he has always taken a very (keen)[76] interest in whatever of beauty and wild nature still survives in and about London. He more than anyone else was instrumental in saving the Old Deer Park from desecration after the Government had actually given their consent for the erection of the Physical Laboratory there.[77] By now it would have been covered with buildings, and I hope this great service he rendered to London will never be forgotten.

On the publication of my book on London Birds[78] Major Wheatley who was then the Head Official of the Woods and Forests asked me to draw up a paper of suggestions as to the best means of encouraging bird life in the Parks. I sent him the paper, containing many suggestions, but the only one acted on was the planting of beds of sedges in the Serpentine and some other ornamental waters – including Pen Ponds. I don't think there was any real desire – certainly no enthusiasm – to do anything of importance in the matter.

The weather here has been so incessantly rough and wet that I have had no outings for many days: I struggle on with my work, and was sorry to see a paragraph in yesterday's *Times* about my *Lost British Birds* as I don't know when I shall be able to do it. I have other things to do that come before it and little strength to work.[79]

PART II

Letters to
Mrs Emma Hubbard
& Mrs Eliza Phillips

Unlike Part I the texts that follow are mainly extracts. In all cases the opening and closing salutations have been omitted. Letters to Mrs Hubbard all began 'Dear Mrs Hubbard', and generally closed with 'Yours sincerely'. To Mrs Phillips he began 'Dear Mrs Phillips', and closed with 'Yours very truly'.

His letters to both ladies were always signed 'W. H. Hudson'.

I

Thank you very much for sending me the raven story: it is extremely interesting and affords a good example of the muddle sometimes resulting from a mixture of intellect with instinct. The immediate cause of the sitting rage in birds is supposed to be a peculiar condition of irritability in the nerves on the surface of the belly which nothing will sooth but the round polished balls of the eggs in the nest. The raven is one of the species in which both sexes take their share in incubation, and the male is probably in the same condition as the female and must have eggs to sit on. The curious point is the 'taking strength' of the bird in getting pebbles as a substitute for eggs. Mr Ernest Hart[1] told me a story of his pet raven which seems more wonderful. The bird sat on his garden wall and watched his next door neighbour bedding out some plants – onions I think they were; and after the man had finished the work and gone away, the raven set to work, pulled them all up one by one and replanted them in a bed in his owner's (Hart's) garden!

Letters telling strange things of the rook appeared some time ago in *Nature* – probably you saw them.

I have not been very well lately since I returned about three weeks ago from Hampshire, where I had a long ramble in Alice Holt and Wolmer Forests. I fear the silent season will be on us before I shall be able to get away again.

———————————

2

(*13 September 1896 to Mrs Phillips from 40 St Lukes Road, W.*)

The letter from Eastbourne reminds me of what I said to you several weeks ago – when you first spoke of the peregrines at Seaford – that it would be a good thing perhaps to draw up a remonstration, or rather a letter, to the Sussex County Council urging them to take steps to preserve their wild birds. I even had it in my mind to propose it at the committee meeting: I did nothing possibly because this physical worry which will not let me rest has made me somewhat 'weak in the intellectuals'. It is certainly making me very timid – of myself and others as well. If you think anything of it I will write a draft letter containing some things which might be said on the subject and send it to you for suggestions, and we could then forward it to Mr Sharpe[2] who knows most about dealing with county councils; and get it ready to submit to the committee at the October meeting. To draw up a proper final letter I should have to consult Borrer[3] and other authorities on Sussex birds to make sure of facts etc, and for this should have to wait for the reopening of the Zoological Library.[4] It is always closed during September.

You kindly hope that I am 'bearing up against all this rain'. Why the rain is my very good friend. I doubt if much of it tells against anyone's health as excessive dryness does, or cold, or heat. I should be badly off without the rain in this melancholy time. My worrying heart prevents me from sleeping at night, and the rain, sounding very loud on this flat zinc roof so close overhead, and rushing and gurgling in the gutters just outside the open window, as I had it nearly all last night, keeps me company, and is the only sound that tells me of Nature. All that rippling, rushing, gurgling is just as grateful as when heard among mountain torrents, or among woodlands, when the Mother of Months
'Fills the shadows and windy places
With lisp of leaves and ripple of rain'.

3

(1 September 1897 to Mrs Phillips from 40 St Lukes Road, W.)

If you are reading the magazines perhaps you have seen my 'Wolmer Forest' in *Longman's*, August ?[5] It has brought me one letter of considerable interest which I enclose. The post card is in reply to a long letter I wrote to Mr Whitburn explaining that the question of Wolmer Forest must be included in a general bird protection scheme for the county of Hampshire; that the influential people of Hampshire must be the prime movers in obtaining an Order; and that I am doing what I can in my small way by writing to the Hampshire people I know on the subject.

Mr Kelsall[6] (who has just been offered and has accepted the living of Milton near Christchurch) will do all in his power to keep the question of protecting the birds in Hampshire alive.

I have also had some correspondence lately with a Mr . . .[7]. Alas! it is of small use his vexing his soul at the destruction of the lyre bird of the Australian bush when the extermination of rare birds goes merrily on under his very nose on the Broads. He tells me that ten marsh harriers have been shot this summer: and that is one of the rare species we desire to preserve. Again, he implores me not to say that another specimen exists in Norfolk, since if its existence there becomes known it will be immediately exterminated by collectors! What a state of things! Cowardice – moral cowardice is partly to blame for it. If these Norfolk bird-lovers would openly denounce by name the wealthy private collectors who pay for the rare birds that are killed a change would take place. But they are afraid; as Mr . . .[8] himself told me, 'they are great men and we can't afford to make enemies of them.' Some day if I live a little longer – another year or so, I may be able to strike a better delivered blow at these selfish wretches who are robbing the country of one of its best possessions.

I am glad to hear from Mr . . .[9] that an effort will be made next year to get an extention of the close time for Norfolk. How the framers of their Bird-protection Order came to omit so necessary a thing I can't understand. I am just writing to Mr [Luttrell] of the Somerset County Council urging him to get an extention to September 1st if possible for this county.

Mr Robinson, editor of the Sussex paper, has just written to invite me to go and see him. Unfortunately I cannot do so, and he does not say what he wants to see me about – perhaps he is desirous of bringing some pressure on the West Sussex County Council.

4

(31 December 1898 to Mrs Hubbard from Bournemouth)

I have seen Wallace[10] and the crossbills and shall go from here tomorrow morning to Roydon House, Boldre, Lymington, but do not know how long I shall stay; I should like to stay a week. But it will depend on whether there will be any need for me to go up to town or not. I shall be glad to get away as I have not felt well nor comfortable owing to this worry of rheumatism and to poor Dr Geikie[11] being so down in health, and finally to the cold. It has been intense, and in the house I can't get warm. The house is nice but the fires are – well, they merely serve to make you think that it would be a delightful experience to sit down and get a proper warm.

I went yesterday to see Wallace, and we had a long talk and agreed on the subject of locomotion but disagreed about the migration of birds. Today I am going to Christchurch to meet Mr Kelsall,[12] the vicar of Milton, and together we are going to invade Mr Hart.[13]

I think we have had two fine half-days since I came, and I spent most of the time watching the crossbills. I was no sooner in the place than I began to hear their peculiar sharp clear chirps. They are quite common and as tame as a London wood pigeon. On Thursday I watched one for half an hour feeding on pine cones not six feet above the heads of the people passing under the low tree growing on the sidewalk. The bird paid no attention to the people, and no one passer-by raised his eyes to the bird.

I can't write as this is an uncomfortable pen so must leave the story of other things to some other time. I wish I had your ready pen, and I wish that you could have been there to watch the crossbills with me. The ordinary human being is the blindest, deafest, dullest of all the brutes.

If I can stay a few days at Roydon House I shall let you know.

5

(27 February [1899] to Mrs Hubbard from 40 St Lukes Road, W.)

Thank you for your interesting letter, but I do hope you will now forget about my miserable gloves. If those of yours were not so astonishingly warm and comfortable I should enclose them in this letter, but I shall keep them to be returned when I make my next visit.[14]

Yes, you can describe the single pink or twink chaffinch note,[15] but not the airy laughing rapid notes of the swallow when he sings: but there is something wrong here: his anger and alarm cry is shrill – piercing almost – and was rightly described as the shrill swallow's cry. But the song is the opposite of shrill: the quality is very pure and curiously reminds one of a fine contralto voice made fine and thin, if a contralto *can* be made thin. But thin or not – it has the tenderness, the feeling of that voice in women.

It is the same with me, always I am thinking of things it would be interesting to discuss with you – I am rather given to sucking brains – but there never appears to be time for it. You must try to arrange a week in the country in some spot so wild and desolate that it will please us both, so that we may be together and discuss a good number of subjects in arrears – a marsh for preference. Thoreau[16] says I enter a marsh as I do a sacred place.

6

(7 June [1899] to Mrs Hubbard from Seaford)

I came down on Monday and had a long walk towards Beachy Head and watched the herring gulls at their breeding place on the cliffs. There was no one there but myself, and after I had comfortably settled down to watch the birds they too began to settle down near me in pairs or groups of three or four, and their white figures among the glowing patches of sea-pink looked wonderfully beautiful.

Yesterday I had a dip in the sea at six in the morning and then started for a long day's walk over the downs. I got to the villages of Firle and Glynde and came back by Lewes, but the day was frightfully hot. About eleven o'clock I was so consumed with thirst that I went nearly half a mile out of my way – a cart track over the downs – to interview a shepherd standing watching his flock near an old half-ruined stone building. He showed me an old well near the spot, but said that unless I had a bottle and a long string I could not get any water. However, my tweed hat fastened to the crook of my stick served as a bucket, and after drinking a hatful of cold water I felt refreshed.[17]

You lose a great deal by not being able to go over these downs; yet it seems to me that it would be impossible to enjoy them in any way but by walking over them; and that you cannot do because you have got a heart. And yet we consider it a reproach to say of a person that he is without a heart! I wonder if you have the feeling that nature cannot be enjoyed in and from a carriage or vehicle of any kind. I can enjoy everything on horseback, but alas! the possessor of a horse, even a broken down old screw, wants to make a fortune out of him, and so I may not ride.

This morning I got out before eight o'clock and so have been over twelve hours on foot. I went over the downs to Beachy Head and paid a visit to the learned shepherd, Stephen Blackmore, who collects flint implements. Poor old fellow, he is getting rather feeble, and no wonder after seventy years of labour, a one armed man, living on twelve shillings a week!

I walked back by the cliff – the Seven Sisters, and I want no more of them! It was dreadful to have to surmount all those seven gigantic downs one after another, anxious to get back before dark. Owing to so much up and down I think my sixteen mile walk was as good as twenty miles. On the way I saw wheatears – males in their beautiful summer dress, and I was sorry not to be able to spend an hour watching them in the hope of hearing their song notes.[18] About their music there is a question, as it seems that no living ornithologist knows the song. It is really curious how the chats – birds with sweet voices – are so silent. But it is the same with the wagtails: one wonders why they have a song.

Tomorrow I think of going to Jevington, near Eastbourne, for a few days and should be delighted to have a letter from you there,

addressed to the Post Office. Jevington is a small pretty rustic village among great downs, and near it are some of the best spots to see the flowers and creatures characteristic of the South Downs.

I wonder if you can tell me what the enclosed flower is? It is very pretty – deep, almost maroon, red flowers in a big coarse burdock-like plant. It is not in my book, Step's *Wayside and Woodland Blossoms*.[19] Today I found the pretty graceful dropwort just opening. I wonder if a box of the big flowers and leaves of the downs would reach you with any life in them? I should like to send you a collection.

7

(²⁰*[1899]* to *Mrs Hubbard from Sea View, Goring, Sussex*)

It seems a long time since we exchanged letters: when you last wrote you were going to R. Pk.[21] with Miss Paget. I think your visit was to be on the one really splendid day we have had – here at all events. That day I had a good walk, and got to Jevington where I dined with the good people I stayed with some time ago; then I went to Willingdon and back to Jevington to tea, and at the finish of that function it was gloomy and evening coming on, and five miles over the downs to walk. I got to Seaford in rain and darkness at half past eight, having been out twelve and a half hours!

At Seaford nothing interesting happened, except wind and storm, and a dead shrew which I picked up one day. A poor miserable-looking wild bullfinch in a cage in the kitchen where I stayed was a constant vexation to me, so when I left on Monday morning I persuaded the woman to part with it for a trifle and took it with me in a perforated cardboard box to Lewes. Then I carried it into some private grounds where the Priory ruins are, and masses of ivy, and old trees, and water and other good things, and liberated it. For half an hour I watched it revelling in the grass vigorously pecking at every green thing, and flying about loudly chirping, or piping, expressing its joy at having been rescued from its Devil's Island.[22]

Then I walked on the crest of the downs to Ditchling, talking with a shepherd or two on the way; then took train at Hassocks to Worthing. I slept there last night, and visited a Mr Fletcher, a gentleman of means who has made the British Lepidoptera a life-long study. His butterflies are really beautiful although dead. This season he has reared scores of deaths head moths and has some just hatched out. They were lovely to look at in their soft clouded grey and rich yellow, and as they walked about over us, kept up a constant squeaking.[23] On my telling Mr F. that I had been looking for the insect in the potatoe patches in order to watch its motions and hear it squeak as it flies, he laughed and said it was a vain quest: he *never* sees the insect flying and thinks it exceedingly rare in a perfect state although abundant in the pupa form. He gets an unlimited supply of chrysalids from the men who dig up the potatoes hereabouts.

Mr F. is also interested in vipers and has given me a queer photograph of five vipers in his hand, taken by his son. I send it for you to see and to keep for me. He catches the vipers and tames them. He says that always after four or five days they become ridiculously tame and can then be handled with impunity. He takes them up in bunches and lets them wind about his fingers. This is strange to me, and I am inclined to believe that he has some magnetism in his hands that produces a soothing effect on the creatures.

I came here this morning thinking that it might be a good place to stay a few days in. On arriving I enquired for Jefferies'[24] cottage, and found that it is almost the only one in the place where rooms may be had, and that the rooms were all vacant; so I at once settled to remain until Saturday next.

Sea View is a large well built comfortable cottage in its own grounds, ivied and pleasant to look at, with fig and apple trees in the grounds; the sea close by. There are two very nice sitting-rooms and kitchen on the ground floor, and two floors above. My bed-room on the first floor, with a view of the sea, is the one Jefferies occupied, but he died downstairs in one of the sitting-rooms. In the garden there is a now ruinous summer house where he often sat to do his writing. The people of this cottage did not know him as they came here ten years ago, after his death.

But I can't post a letter tonight as this is a small dark peaceful village out of which the post goes early, and it is now growing late. I was so tired last night with my long walk over the high windy

70

downs, and my ramble in the evening at Worthing looking for a
shelter, that when I did find one I could not sleep, at least until the
wee sma' hours: so now I feel very done up. And so I shall wish you
goodnight and finish this tomorrow.

A rainy morning! But I slept soundly, and poor R.J.'s ghost
did not disturb me – they seldom come back. I wish they did. I
forgot to tell you that as I came here yesterday afternoon we had
a tremendous thunder storm, and a deluge of rain. I took shelter
in the church porch.[25]

Please write a line and tell me what you think about Burnham
Beeches.[26] I want to go there with you if you can say the time.
When does colour come, do you know? Pardon this long screed.

8

*(27 May 1900 to Mrs Hubbard from Roydon House, Lyming-
ton,[27] Hampshire)*

After all my Sussex rambles among old picturesque buildings
I see Roydon once more as the ideal beautiful house – a wonderful
gem of red brick in its green and flowery setting. And the birds are
wonderful. No cat or dog to frighten them; the shyest ones have
become tame. In a yew close to the front door a bullfinch has a
nest full of young; and a couple of yards from the bullfinch a
bottle-tit[28] has a round nest as big as a coconut hanging from a
yew twig. You can look into it and see the mother sitting on her
young. Close by a robin is sitting on a cuckoo's egg; and as for
thrushes, blackbirds and starlings one could fill half a bushel with
the young birds in the small garden. In the evening you hear owls
hooting, nightjars reeling and woodcock grunting and whistling.
Last evening I watched several woodcock fly above close to the
house.

The weather is lovely just now, and I hope you will have it as
fine when you start. I do hope you will get to Droxford – that discovery of old bones and weapons is exceedingly interesting. The
other family I know here, living close by – millers and farmers – I

find are from Droxford. Mrs Tarle, the wife, says she was born there. Her father was a farmer named Goore, strange to say. When I told her about the discovery of bones she said that her father's shepherd over twenty years ago found some human skeletons very near the surface, and that they were taken and buried in the churchyard. He was prodding the ground with the iron point of his crook and struck a hard object and dug down to see what it was, and so discovered the bones.

Yesterday afternoon I ran over to Brockenhurst to get a paper, and by a lucky chance caught sight of my friend Mr Kelsall[29] (Vicar of Milton) flying off on his bike. I shouted and brought him to, and he was astonished to see me, and came to Roydon to see the nests and talk about birds, so we had a couple of delightful hours together.

9

(30 May [1900] to Mrs Hubbard from Roydon House, Lymington)

Very many thanks for your interesting letter: I am sorry you are not going to see Droxford this time, but hope there will be much to interest you at other spots, especially at Stratford. The most interesting sight I saw there was a magpie sitting on a grave-stone in Stratford churchyard. He looked like a very beautiful bird carved out of white marble and jet. I daresay you will think it was a pity that big ugly vulgar theatre was stuck up in the town.

The cuckoo hatched on Sunday afternoon, and yesterday – when the hours of his life numbered thirty-six – the whole business of getting the entire nest and attention of the old birds to himself was accomplished. He did it all very well, and as I witnessed it I must send a note of it to one of the Natural History Papers – the *Field* probably.[30] It is funny to think that two years ago Wallace[31] asked me to try and see the process so as to set the question at rest. But of course there is no question after Mrs Blackburn's account in her *Bird from Moidart*[32] confirming Jenner's facts.

I told you of bullfinch and bottle-tit with nests and young

72

close to the front door. I did not know then that another rare beauty had his cradle nest within about three yards of the bull-finch's nest – the golden crested wren. I heard his squeaky song near the door, and there to the nest is so low that you can bend the ivy it is suspended to and look into it. The bird is sitting on four eggs, and when I pull down the branch she looks startled but doesn't go off unless I make her. A little fairy of a bird, with eggs like little pills – not Carters.[33] The common wren, too, has a nest near the door, and a little further away there is a nest of the chaffinch. But enough of birds for this time.

Rollstone[34] – *Evening*

I broke off having suddenly made up my mind to run over to Beaulieu. From there I went to Otterwood and had lunch with the owner, and looked for and found the Dartford warblers. Then I came on here, and am going to stay the night. It is nearly closing time of the post at Fawley so shall conclude this in haste. I think I shall be at Roydon to Saturday.

<hr>

I O

(*14 June* [*1900*] *to Mrs Hubbard from Rollstone, Fawley, Southampton*)

I came over here two days ago and was glad to get a letter from you this morning. I should like immediately to pay you a visit, but your time at Selborne is very short – I had thought it was to be a considerably longer stay – and I fear I shall not be fit for the thirty mile run. Southampton is a rather difficult place to get at from this side; but that is a small matter. The trouble is I have not felt, and am not yet feeling, well; my heart will 'palpitate' and I feel as tired as if I had been doing a vast amount of exercise. Still I think I should venture to say 'yes' if I could make sense of my Gladstone.[35] I believe it at Beaulieu Road Station, but it was not there yesterday when the cart went with butter and eggs; and I do not know whether it will reach me this week. And without it

73

I cannot stir as I need the clothes in it. All things considered it will be safest to say that you must not expect me, but if I find it possible to go I shall be very glad indeed to pay you a visit.

It is a little late to see and hear the birds: but just here there is a greater abundance of life than at most places, and so I hear a good deal, altho' not nearly so much as in May!

I have heard and seen a pair of greater spotted woodpeckers better than on any previous occasion; and the nightingales here are still singing – there were three singing last evening on the edge of the rick yard; and yet there are young ones out of the nest. They look like young robins, but are browner. Every evening I see as well as hear the nightjars, and hear but do not see the brown owls. Just before sunset yesterday I listened to a jay singing one of his songs one seldom hears – three musical notes, followed by a long soft trill.

At Roydon House, on Monday last, the cuckoo was still flourishing like a green bay tree. He is big now, and barred like a hawk, and if you offer him a worm he swells up and hisses and pecks most savagely at the hand. The bottle-tits came out and went away to the wood, so we cut the twig with the round nest fastened to it and put it up as an ornament in the hall. The bull-finches, too, left the nest, and one of them flew into the hall and sat there until found and put back in the tree.

Here at Rollstone a fowl, a duck, a guinea fowl and a red-legged partridge all laid in one nest near the house. The duck in the end turned all the others out, and is now sitting on the partridge's eggs, the others having been taken from her.

I I

(*24 June* [*1900*] *to Mrs Hubbard from Rollstone, Fawley, Southampton*)

I am not sure that Autumn would be a good season for a visit to Selborne: to see beautiful woodland scenery and beeches in the splendor of autumnal tints I think you would find Midhurst or

Harting, or somewhere in sight or reach of the West Sussex Downs a better place. Beech trees hardly exist here, but it is glorious with oaks: I never saw them in such perfection as they are at Beaulieu – the greenness is beyond one's power to imagine or to describe.

But the best time goes too quick – too quickly, and the nightingale has the reputation of the first to cease singing of all our woodland songsters. He is not earlier than others. They *all* cease singing during the last half of June. I mean all species: individuals sing here and there and now and then. Occasionally you hear a nightingale at the end of June, or in July. But for one nightingale there are forty blackbirds, and fifty willow wrens, and sixty chaffinches. And that is the reason why these and other common species are heard after nightingales have dropped into silence.

The Greys[36] want me to go on Saturday next, and as Highwood,[37] Romsey, is on the way I am thinking of leaving here about Thursday so as to take the two places in one trip, then getting back to Brockenhurst or going on to London – I have not yet settled which will be best. I hope to be well enough to cycle by Thursday or Friday. At present I do not feel quite well: last night I could not sleep at all, and my throat keeps rough, but I may be better in a few days.

About the birds ceasing their singing: I was going to say that in spite of that growing silence (so far as pure singing goes) the woods teem with interesting sights and sounds at present. Yesterday afternoon I went into the King Copse, the nearest point to the house, and seeing a half-dead tree where a spotted woodpecker has been at work, I stood still thinking the bird might show himself if I waited a few minutes. He did not appear, but in those few minutes a wren scolded me, then a willow wren, then a woodwren. A squirrel coughed and chattered and ran about on an oak tree and watched me. A green woodpecker laughed somewhere. A party of young jays, not long out, sat on a bough quite near, and twice the old birds came and fed them, the old ones screaming, and the young ones making all sorts of strange noises; and last but not least a pair of kestrels sailed about, and two or three times brought food to their young in a nest at the top of a fir tree. I could hear the shrill piping of the young, while the old birds at intervals burst out in screams of shrill laughter – a most hysterical cry! After waiting twenty minutes I turned away, and coming out of the shade of the trees disturbed a fine ring-snake which I caught to look at. It was beautiful to see the cobra-like way in which he

75

expanded his neck and anterior part of the body. The adders of which I have seen a good number, and the smooth snake (to judge from the one I caught and examined) have not that serpent trick of flattening the body to twice its usual width.

Yesterday when I sent a hasty line I thought I had dozens of interesting things to write about but I was mistaken or else they have slipped out of my memory.

I 2

(28 June 1900 to Mrs Phillips from Roydon House, Lymington)

I left Rollstone yesterday and came here on my bicycle in the afternoon – after wandering about in quest of bird impressions on the Beaulieu Manor Down by the sea, where there is a lake and many herons. Never before yesterday did I see herons *bathe*. They flap and flop like ducks, then lie in the water a few minutes, then flap again, then *sit up* just like a cat or a baby, the water up to the middle of the body where the waist ought to be. It was most curious.

I intended sleeping one night here, and going on this morning to Romsey; but alas! I had a bad night (palpitations) and so must sit still today, and if all right tomorrow morning start early so as to get to Romsey, brush off the dust and then present myself at Highwood.[38]

And on Saturday I am due at the Greys near Winchester[39]; so until *Monday* my address will be Post Office, Itchen Abbas, Alresford, Hants.

13

Tomorrow when I post this I will put (in)[41] a very small spray of the big reddish purple stuff I spoke about. I think it is water agrimony. In fact I am almost sure of it. Do you know the bog bean? It is common here and bears a curious cottony white flower, but it has been long out of bloom. I can send a root for the pond if you haven't got it. I have found what you called the monkey flower at other spots among the rushes, so that it appears to grow here like any wild flower.

The most interesting thing I have to note is the discovery of the cirl bunting's nest. Again they have made it in the little sweet briar hedge round the house, on the opposite side of the cottage this time. There are three young birds in it. I think it was a stoat and not the jackdaws that destroyed the former nest. A stoat prowls about the place, and I half think he lives somewhere in the roof. Night before last a brown wood mouse got caught in a small wooden mouse-trap, and the . . .[42] stoat devoured its body, which was all outside the trap, and then half-devoured the trap itself in his efforts to get the little head which was shut inside. This morning I caught another wood mouse, a pretty little creature of a bright chestnut colour; and he at once took bread and holding it up in his paws like a squirrel set to and ate it. He escaped in a short time.

A good many birds come about the cottage, and no wonder as there is no cat or dog, and all is so quiet. One young blackbird, an orphan no doubt, and not yet a good flyer, has become quite domestic, and runs to us when we go on to the lawn, and takes what we give him. But he prefers worms, and if I take the trowel and begin to dig the mould he runs to me to take the worms I may turn up.

Up 'till the fierce gale on Friday we had a great number of swallows and house martins; these mostly disappeared that day and were succeeded by a multitude of sand martins. They spend the whole day hawking about in the shelter of the limes looking like big flies or moths; and then settle on a telegraph-line which runs near the cottage – tho' you can't telegraph from this village. How pretty they look sitting all facing one way in hundreds crowded together on the loose wires! Coming back from church today I found one dead in the field. This little traveller to Africa has not got very far on his journey! He was a young bird and very pretty, even dead. I buried his soft little bird-moth body very deep at the roots of a big honeysuckle that grows at the cottage door.

A white owl comes out in the evening and beats over the rushy ground in the valley before our door. From the lawn we can watch little coot-moorehen-dabchick comedies in the water near. They sometimes quarrel and make a great noise and splashing.

———————————

14

(16 February 1901 to Mrs Phillips from 40 St Lukes Road, W.)

Mr Eagle Clarke who is a rather distinguished ornithologist and is a secretary and getting a good many associates,[43] has sent a long report about the breeding of the pintail in Loch Leven in Kinross. Will you look at my *British Birds*[44] where there is a minute but very good drawing of the pintail duck. It is one of the most beautiful British birds, and a few pairs breed in Ireland, and it *used* to breed in one place in Northumberland. Now in 1898 it was discovered that the bird had established a breeding colony in Loch Leven in the little island in the lake, where many other ducks and birds of different kinds breed. The lake is the property of a Sir . . . Montgomery, Bart,[45] and the fishing rights are let to an anglers' association, and both the owner and the association *forbid* the taking of eggs. But since the discovery of the pintails breeding there was made there has been a rush to take their eggs, the anglers and boatmen conspiring to do it. Mr E. Clarke proposes first to urge the County Council of that county to obtain an order at once for the protection of the eggs; second, to address (from our society),[46] letters to Sir . . . Montgomery and the anglers' association on the subject; and third, *to help* in defraying the cost of a watcher which he (E.C.) will have appointed to keep guard this Spring. This is to be done, and if help in money is wanted we are to give it to the extent of ten pounds. Mr E. Clarke does not know

that any assistance will be wanted after the proprietor and others have been . . .[47] but he is anxious to do something immediately, and to know that he can have help should it be wanted.

It will certainly be a fine thing if we can save this colony, as it will be the beginning of a hatched and bred British race of the bird which will spread over the country. This is indeed what happened in the case of the gadwell, another pretty duck which came to us as a winter visitor and bred occasionally in Scotland and in the North of England, until Lord Walsingham got a few pairs and released them pinioned is his estate in Broadland, and there bred and attracted others, and now the bird breeds largely in that district of Norfolk, and is thoroughly established.

15

(1 October 1901 to Mrs Phillips from 40 St Lukes Road, W.)

Alas, I am the last person in all this populous land to advise you about the ailments of love birds, or any other feathered creature in a cage. I know that caged birds scratch and pull each others' feathers out purely out of kindness. All social animals scratch and rub each other. You have seen a horse say to another horse 'You scratch my back and I'll scratch yours', and at once they proceed to do so – scratching one another with their teeth on the shoulders. Monkeys, too, feeling that they have fleas about them set to work to look for fleas in their neighbour's fur on the same principle. And poor caged birds, infested with mites and other parasites, pluck out each others' feathers. It makes me shiver to see them, and if I must see them then I should prefer to see them dead and at peace – poor little man-tortured beings. I mean if I must see them here in this strange land: but to look on them in their own vast sun-lit forests, tumbling down, a shiny green rain out of a hot blue sky, making the air ring with their shrill glad multitudinous cries – that, they say, is an exhilarating sight. I hope that Lady . . .[48] would prefer that sight to the sight of a humanized love bird in a cage, its feathers plucked out.

16

(2 September 1904 to Mrs Phillips from 40 St Lukes Road, W.)

More haste less speed; if I had not written so briefly and hurriedly yesterday I would have explained what the *swallow* subject was I wished to see Mrs Lemon[49] about. It referred to the decrease of swallows throughout the country. It was the subject I brought forward at the committee meeting, and it was agreed that enquiries should be made as to whether or not wholesale destruction of swallows took place during the autumnal migration in the southern part of France. So far nothing has been done to carry out the resolution of the committee beyond the writing of two or three letters to persons in France and Italy who may possibly know something about the matter. I urged that something more definite should be done; that someone to make enquiries on the spot should be sent by the Society, and I am anxious to know what the Lemons propose to do about it.

But this decrease in the swallow which has continued these ten years past is not affected and has nothing to do with any local persecution the birds may be subjected to by boys in a suburb of London. I am glad to know that such a thing is very exceptional and could only take place in a suburb of London where children are so brutalized by the conditions they exist in. In all the country districts known to me the swallow is regarded by all persons with a peculiar tenderness, almost as a sacred bird. The cause of its decline must therefore be looked for *out of England*, and if as I imagine, it results from large numbers being taken annually in France on migration then there would be a good case to found some action on, and what I suggested was that the Society might represent the matter to the Government and ask that representations be made to the French Government. I said that such an action on our part would be approved of by all persons, and that it would bring the Society and its work before the public. The next committee meeting will not be until October 15 when it will be too late to make any investigations abroad.

17

(*19 September 1904 to Mrs Phillips from Troston, Ixworth, Suffolk*)

I very suddenly made up my mind to get away for a few days, and put a small old forgotten book in my pocket, thinking that I would perhaps be in the neighbourhood of the village where the poor forgotten little poet who wrote it was born. The poor little poet was Robert Bloomfield,[50] and the man who discovered him, and then *boomed* him and made him popular was Capel Lofft – a great personage in literary England a hundred and fifteen or twenty years ago. I daresay the curious name is familiar to you.

I came by train to Brandon on Thursday intending to sleep there – it is the small old Suffolk town where flints to strike fire with are still made. It was such a splendid day that I could not stay, so I rode on my bicycle to Thetford, over six or seven miles of open country of bracken and pine without a house in sight. I saw a stone curlew – it rose up near me by the road.

At Thetford I felt that I would prefer a village for a stopping place and so started off to Honington – the village where Bloomfield was born. I was told of the inn, The Fox, there and assured I could get a bed. But when I got there in the evening, quite tired, they refused me accommodation and said I must go on to the next village – Troston. So at last I arrived here – more tired than ever, and found I could not have a bed at the inn – a shooting gentleman had engaged the one spare room. However I found a place at a carter's cottage and was made quite comfortable.

Next day I went back to Honington[51] to see the village properly, and was told by the landlady of The Fox that she was very sorry not to have told me I could have got a bed at the Rectory! I thought it about the absurdest thing I had ever heard, but have since discovered that it was quite right. The Rector is not only the parson of the parish but the village carrier as well, and drives a cart on market days to Bury St Edmunds and takes parcels and passengers. He stables and grooms his horses, and cultivates his own vegetables and does everything. He'll even give a bed to a stranger! I am sorry to have missed seeing this curious man. But I saw a good many of the cottagers, and it is rather odd that after a hundred years Bloomfield's name should be well known to everyone in the place.

Adjoining Honington – with the pretty little Ouse dividing them – is the village of Sapiston, where Bloomfield worked as a plough-boy at a small farm. There I went and visited the Rector, a learned man, and expected to find him greatly interested in my poor little poet. But he was not! The learned man was in his garden, in his old clothes and very bad boots. He said he had heard of Bloomfield but took no interest in him. He got the key and took me to see the church which stands a long way from the village among the meadows by the river – a very small ancient church. 'Are you an archaeologist or what?' he asked me. I said I was supposed to be a naturalist but took an intelligent interest in churches and most things. Then he told me a story of a nightingale, and an omen. A nightingale sang at the rectory for two or three summers following until 1900, when a strange thing happened. One morning the bird had been singing for a long time in a bush on the lawn near the drawing-room window. His wife was in the room by the window writing. By and by she went to him in the study and said a small bird had dashed itself against the glass three times and then fallen on the steps outside. He at once went to see and found the nightingale lying there, and when he took it up it gasped once or twice and died in his hand. Since then they have had no nightingale sing at the rectory. His wife died that year and he appeared to think or half believe that the tragedy of the bird was a kind of prophesy or premonition – or was in some mysterious way related to what was about to take place.[52]

He then took me in to show me his library – a very poor one for a scholar – and then walked to the gate to see me off. After bidding goodbye he called me back to tell him my name. 'Hudson,' I said, and he remarked 'No relation to the Naturalist in La Plata I suppose.' After being told that I was that person he sat down on the grass and started talking afresh.

At Sapiston I rambled about and went into a good number of cottages and they all seemed pleased to have Bloomfield talked about; . . .

And now I must come back to my delightful little village of Troston and to that once great man, Capel Lofft, who even in his day was abused by some envious persons, and said to be a self-advertising humbug. He was a barrister and a man of letters and when an uncle, Robert Capel, squire of Troston died, he inherited

Troston Hall and large estates here. That's in fact how he came to discover Bloomfield who came from a village only two miles away.

Capel Lofft died in 1825 and was succeeded by a son, who was followed by his son – Robert Evelyn Lofft – the last of the Loffts, who died an old bachelor four years ago. He had a most remarkable life. He was a tall thin man, with long hair, and a great opinion of his own abilities. He quarrelled with all his tenants and had all his farms thrown on to his hands, and he then began farming his own land in a very magnificent way with borrowed money. He bought large numbers of pedigree cattle and built enormous cow-houses close to the Hall, an Elizabethan mansion, and finally ruined himself, and had his house seized by creditors and his furniture and everything sold. He lived his last few years in a cottage in the village, the house having been let. Since his death his estate has been in the market and a short time ago was put up for sale at ...[53] when the highest bid was eighteen thousand pounds. The building cost very much more, and the land alone should be worth sixty thousand pounds. And so the place has no squire now, and the Elizabethan house is empty. Today I spent some hours going over it and through the grounds – park and gardens. It is in the care of a gardener who lives there with his wife and two small children. There are owls about the house and legions of martins who have rows on rows of their mud cradles under the eaves.

Kingfishers are seen in the stream close by, and I was delighted to hear the twitter of goldfinch, or as it is called in Suffolk *King Harry*. A rather good name for the goldfinch. Today while I was with the caretaker and his children at the back of the house, I called their attention to the goldfinches' *twit-twit* in the trees, and while we were listening down came four of them into a thistle-plant growing there and began to feed, the old birds picking at the downy thistle-heads 'till their beaks were full of little seeds, while the young birds perpetually fluttered their wings and called and called 'till they were fed. The children were highly delighted to see the birds with my binocular as it made the little beautiful creatures look as close as their own hands to them. They had never seen a goldfinch in that way before.

I am beginning to feel quite ashamed of the length of this letter. I fear it will be very nearly illegible. 'Tis a nasty paper[54] and a nasty pin-like pen.

From here I shall cycle to Bury St Edmunds and take the train there to London. This afternoon I was at Easton – the village and hall which was burnt down two or three years ago and is being rebuilt. The river flows by the house and I sat there some time watching the birds – several herons, dozens of coot, moorhens and wild duck, and a hundred or more pewits.[55] A charming gathering.

TAILPIECE

A Letter to a
Very Young Lady

This charming letter is probably unique in the sense that, so
far as we know, it is Hudson's only extant letter to a child.[1]

(21 December 1911 to Elsa from 40 St Lukes Road, W.)

My dear Elsa,

I have great pleasure in sending you as a Xmas card a story
of mine about a little boy lost[2] and hope you won't think it perfect
nonsense. I think you said you didn't believe in Fairies. Well I
don't agree with you there, but we needn't argue at Xmas time,
and besides the tale is not absolutely about fairy-land but only
about that borderland between the common world we all know
and that queer place where very curious and funny things happen.

I am going to put in the parcel along with my book a *real*
fairy-tale, told in rhyme by a woman poet. There are no great
women poets and never have been, but they write very charmingly
sometimes, and many people think that Christina Rosetti was the
best lady poet we have ever had in England. And *I* think that
Goblin Market is the loveliest thing she ever wrote. I should like
you to tell me, if you write, whether you like poetry or not.

I hope you have not forgotten our meeting at Littlehampton,
when I took down the address you were staying at. Well, I would

87

have turned up the next morning to ask your mother and you to pay us a visit and have tea with us at our lodgings just by the common, but unhappily my wife got worse that same day and we had to get back to London as soon as we could, and she has been bad ever since and it will be months I'm afraid before she will be able to get out again. However, I hope we shall meet again at some future time and that we will be very good friends and not quarrel about the existence of fairies or anything else.

Please give my best regards to your mother and with all good wishes for the season.

I am yours always

W. H. HUDSON

Notes

INTRODUCTION

1. Later published in book form entitled *Letters on the Ornithology of Buenos Ayres* by W. H. Hudson, edited by David R. Dewar (Cornell University Press, 1951).
2. *The Naturalist in La Plata* by W. H. Hudson (Chapman and Hall, 1892).
3. *Idle Days in Patagonia* by W. H. Hudson (Chapman and Hall, 1893).
4. *Birds of La Plata* by W. H. Hudson, Vols I and II (Dent, 1920).
5. *A Hind in Richmond Park* by W. H. Hudson (Dent, 1922), 'Conclusions'. It was the last book Hudson wrote and it was published posthumously.
6. *The Book of a Naturalist* by W. H. Hudson (Hodder and Stoughton, 1919), Chapter 14.
7. *The Book of a Naturalist*, Chapter 14.
8. Sir Edward Grey (later Viscount Grey of Fallodon). (1862–1933). Member of Parliament for Berwick-on-Tweed and Secretary of State for Foreign Affairs from 1905 to 1916.
9. Parliamentary Papers (1902), LV, p. 133.
10. *Nature in Downland* by W. H. Hudson (Longmans, 1900).
11. *A Shepherd's Life* by W. H. Hudson (Methuen, 1910).
12. *Hampshire Days* by W. H. Hudson (Longmans, 1903).
13. Unpublished letter to Mrs Phillips of 4 June 1905.
14. Unpublished letter to Mrs Phillips of 25 October 1893.
15. *Birds in Town and Village* by W. H. Hudson (Dent, 1919), essay 'The Eagle and the Canary'.
16. The Book of Job Chapter 5, Verse 23.

PART ONE: LETTERS TO J. R. HARDING

1. Hudson's home in Westbourne Park, London, now in the postal district of Notting Hill. He sometimes referred to it as 'Tower House'.

2. *British Birds* by W. H. Hudson (Longmans, 1895). It was Hudson's second book about birds in Britain and was written 21 years after he came to England.
3. *Birds and Man* by W. H. Hudson (Longmans, 1901). Chapter XII is entitled 'The Dartford Warbler'. Hudson subsequently updated and rearranged this book and the new edition was published by Duckworth in 1915, its frontispiece being a coloured illustration of a Dartford warbler.
4. Selborne in Hampshire, the former home of Gilbert White (1720–93), author of *The Natural History of Selborne* which Hudson first read when he was 16 years of age in Argentina and which undoubtedly influenced his own writings.
5. Hudson wrote about these swallows in Northbrook Street, Newbury, in Chapter IX of his book *Afoot in England* (Hutchinson, 1909). The incident took place in 1901.
6. After 'how' in this line Hudson had written 'it came about that' but had put a line through it. I have added the word 'arose' merely so that the sentence may be understood in the way that I am sure he intended it.
7. Perhaps Kensington Gardens.
8. Hudson had written a book about London's birds entitled *Birds in London* (Longmans, 1898). It is also a valuable record of London's parks and open spaces at that time.
9. Probably *A History of British Birds* by Henry Seebohm, 2nd Ed, (Nimmo, 1896).
10. *Snipe and Woodcock* by L. H. de V. Shaw *et al* (Longmans, 1903).
11. Hudson was gathering material for, and writing, *The Land's End*, his book about West Cornwall, which was published by Hutchinson in 1908.
12. See Chapter I of *Hampshire Days* by W. H. Hudson (Longmans, 1903).
13. *Birdwatching* by Edmund Selous (Dent, 1901).
14. Hudson was perhaps referring to *Pictures in Prose* by A. B. R. Trevor-Battye, published in 1893.
15. All place-names mentioned in this letter are in south Wiltshire.
16. The water ouzel is now listed as the 'dipper'.
17. A South American Bird of the *Rupicola* family.
18. Hudson was a Fellow of the Zoological Society of London.
19. *The Saturday Review.*
20. When Queen Victoria presented these grounds adjoining Kew Gardens to her people at the time of her Diamond Jubilee they were wooded and overgrown and therefore a magnificent sanctuary for wildlife. A proposal to permit the public to wander freely in them so horrified Hudson who could see how the birds and animals would be disturbed, that he wrote to *The Times* and suggested that people

should be confined to designated paths or walks. His letter was published on 12 April 1898, and his suggestion ultimately adopted.

21. Sir William Thiselton-Dyer, Director of Kew Gardens.

22. 'Aves' by W. H. Hudson ('Royal Botanic Gardens Kew Bulletin of Miscellaneous Information' Additional Series V, 1906).

23. Probably 'In a Green Land' published in *The Saturday Review* in four parts, on 26 June and 6, 20 and 27 July 1912: subsequently collected in his book *Adventures Among Birds* (Hutchinson, 1913).

24. This account of the Dartford warbler appeared in Hudson's article entitled 'In a Green Land' (Part III) which was printed in *The Saturday Review* of 20 July 1912, and which, with little alteration to the wording, he included in Chapter XVII of his book *Adventures Among Birds*. In the magazine article the words he used about Harding were:

> 'It happened that about a year or fourteen months before a friend wrote to inform me that by chance he had discovered a new locality for the Dartford Warbler . . . he was cycling in the south country and when going by a side-road at the edge of a wide heath or moor caught sight of a pair flitting among some furze bushes. He had never previously seen the bird, but I was satisfied that he was right in his identification – that he was about the last man to make a mistake in such a matter. I may add that this same keen observer is not known to me personally; we correspond, and having the same feeling about birds are naturally friends. He is not known as an ornithologist: he is one of those strange but not very uncommon persons who lead a double life. To the theatre-going public he is a finished actor, and those who know him only in his impersonations would, I imagine, hear with surprise, perhaps incredulity, that off the boards, he is a haunter of silent, solitary places where birds inhabit, that in these communings he has a joy with which the playgoer inter-meddleth not.'

25. Hudson described the song of the marsh warbler in Chapter XXI of his book *Adventures Among Birds*.

26. *Adventures Among Birds, op. cit.*

27. 'Wild Wings' (Literary Causerie of the Week) by W. H. Hudson in *The Speaker* of 11 November 1905. The passage which he quoted was, 'utmost Kilda's lonely isle', which in the *final* (ie, 1746) form of James Thomson's poem *The Seasons* reads, 'utmost Kilda's shore'. ('Spring', Line 757). Hudson had first read *The Seasons* in his youth in Argentina.

28. Hudson was bilingual and spoke Spanish probably as fluently as he spoke English.

29. Chapter XXVII of *Adventures Among Birds*.

30. *The Naturalist in La Plata* by W. H. Hudson (Chapman and Hall, 1892).
31. *Idle Days in Patagonia* by W. H. Hudson (Chapman and Hall, 1893).
32. *Adventures Among Birds.*
33. Although Hudson clearly spells 'Lawrence' with a 'w' it was doubtless Laurence Irving (1871–1914), Sir Henry Irving's younger son, who wrote the English version of *Typhoon* by Melchior Lengyel.
34. An ardent campaigner against vivisection. Hudson wrote of her to Edward Garnett on 24 August 1913: 'I know Miss Lind and have the deepest respect for her noble courage when she fought the whole gang of vivisectors and their millionaire patron'. (*153 Letters from W. H. Hudson*, edited etc. by Edward Garnett; Nonesuch Press, 1923.)
35. Evidently in Richmond Park, London: see Letter 17 of 15 June [1913].
36. The Miss Jerrold he refers to is the actress Mary Jerrold (1877–1955), and, according to *The Times* of 2 December 1913, the play being performed at The Queen's Theatre was *If we had only known.*
37. At the beginning of 1913 Hudson, then in his seventy-third year, had a bad heart attack, and though he lived for another eight years he was no longer able to bicycle or walk long distances.
38. Previously Hudson had used the formal salutation 'Dear *Mr* Harding'. Now, after corresponding for eight years, he had dropped formalities and addressed his correspondent as 'Dear Harding'.
39. This friend was Lady Margaret Brooke, the Ranee of Sarawak, wife of Sir Charles Johnson Brooke G.C.M.G., the second white Rajah of Sarawak. She had been his valued friend since 1904.
40. The Ranee of Sarawak.
41. World War I had broken out on 4 August the previous year (1914) and Harding was now serving with the British Red Cross Society.
42. Hudson, though no warmonger, believed that people and nations degenerated during long periods of peace. However the full horror of a war of this magnitude had not yet become apparent to him.
43. *The Story of my Heart: My Autobiography* by the Wiltshire rural writer, Richard Jefferies (Longmans, 1883).
44. From December 1917 until the end of his life Hudson spent each winter in Penzance where he occupied these same rooms.
45. In 1894 Hudson had written a 32-page pamphlet for The (Royal) Society for the Protection of Birds entitled *Lost British Birds* in which he listed the bittern and wrote:

    'This species, once called the common bittern, and found in all suitable localities in England, Scotland and Ireland, was one of the most fascinating of the British birds on account of its solitary, mysterious habits, its strange richly coloured and beautifully pencilled plumage, and that booming cry, once familiar in our land, that "shakes the sounding marsh". This "boom", which was uttered during the love season, is likened by those who have heard it to the deep-toned bellowing of a bull. People wondered how so vast a volume of sound could proceed from a bird of its size; and superstitious persons, who dwelt commonly within hearing of it, attributed the sound to no bittern, or bird, but to the demon or spirit of the desolate places of the earth.'

46. John Davidson (1857–1909), the poet and playwright, who in a fit of depression drowned himself in Mount's Bay in 1909 (*see also* Letter 32).

47. The first edition of *A Shepherd's Life* by W. H. Hudson (Methuen, 1910).

48. 'Caleb Bawcombe' whose real name was James Lawes, the central character in Hudson's *A Shepherd's Life* (*see* Chapter 7 of *W. H. Hudson: Writer and Naturalist* by Dennis Shrubsall; Compton Press, 1978). Lawes died in 1914.

49. Hudson's paternal grandfather was a Devonian from Clyst Hydon, some eight miles north-east of Exeter, and Hudson often referred to Exeter as his 'natal city'.

50. Hudson was not so much worried about the influenza itself but about the consequential damage to his weak heart.

51. Morley Charles Roberts, the novelist (1857–1942). Hudson first met him in 1880 and they remained close friends for 42 years until Hudson's death.

52. The 1:50,000 Ordnance Survey Map, First Series (1974) shows the spelling as 'Peper Harow': Black's *Guide to Surrey* (1887), third edition, gives it as 'Peperharrow'.

53. *Far Away and Long Ago: A History of my Early Life* by W. H. Hudson (Dent, 1918).

54. See Letters 26 and 32.

55. Thomas Edward Brown (1830–97), poet.

56. Michael Drayton's (1563–1631) long poem about the topographical features (particularly rivers) and history of England which he finished in 1622.

57. Alfred Noyes (1880–1958). British poet.

58. Hudson omitted the day date.

59. Probably J. E. Harting, author of *Birds of Middlesex* (1866), the same ornithologist to whom Hudson refers on pages 2, 179 and 307 of his *Birds in London* (Longman's, 1898).

60. Although during September of the following year (1921) Dent published Hudson's *A Traveller in Little Things* – a little under half of which had already appeared in magazines – Hudson is doubtless

referring to his last book, *A Hind in Richmond Park*, which was published posthumously by Dent in November 1922.

61. *Dead Man's Plack*, his story of the Saxon King Edgar's murder of his friend, Earl Athewold, in Harewood Forest, Hampshire. Hudson was very familiar with the area, and the spot where the murder is believed to have been committed is still marked with a stone cross. Together with another of Hudson's 'long short stories' it was published in a book entitled *Dead Man's Plack and An Old Thorn* (Dent, 1920).

62. The autobiography of his boyhood first published by Dent in 1918.

63. His romantic fiction set in Guyana in which he related the adventures of a young Venezuelan gentleman and Rima, a beautiful girl who lived close to nature in a forest. The book was first published by Duckworth in 1904, but its real success came in 1916 when Alfred Knopf brought out an edition in U.S.A. which contained an Introduction by Hudson's friend, the famous novelist, John Galsworthy. The story was made into a film by M.G.M. (released in 1959), in which the role of the heroine was played by Audrey Hepburn.

64. A book of 29 essays – mainly about mammals, reptiles, birds and insects – only eight of which had not previously appeared as articles in magazines. The book was first published by Hodder and Stoughton in 1919.

65. Hudson omitted the day date.

66. Sir Peter Chalmers Mitchell (1864–1945 – Knighted 1929) was secretary of the Zoological Society of London from 1903 to 1935.

67. Harding had asked Hudson if he could suggest to whom the vale at Long Ditton was sacred as related by John Davidson (see letter 26) in the following lines:

'Once in June
Upstream I went to hear the summertime,
The birds sing at Long Ditton in a vale
Sacred to him who wrote his own heart's tale.

———

High in the oak trees where the fresh leaves sprout,
The blackbirds with their oboe voices make
The sweetest broken music . . .'

68. See Letter 26.

69. *Birds in a Village* (Chapman and Hall, 1893). It was Hudson's first nature book about England, and was written at a time when he greatly needed some encouragement.

70. Mrs Hudson died in Worthing, West Sussex, on 19 March 1921, and this letter was written on black-edged notepaper.

71. His last book, *A Hind in Richmond Park*. Hudson, in fact, started work on it during the summer of 1918, and when he died on 18

August 1922 it was still unfinished. The substance of the last five pages, though drafted, had not been arranged, so his old friend Morley Roberts (*see* Note 51) finished it. It was published by Dent in November 1922.

72. Not currently listed. Hudson is evidently referring to the common tern.

73. Hudson had been a member of the Council of the Royal Society for the Protection of Birds for many years and had, in fact, proposed Harding's election to it. The invitation was extended in the R.S.P.B.'s letter of 14 November 1921, signed by Frank E. Lemon, the honorary secretary of the Society.

74. Hudson died six months later, on 18 August 1922.

75. H.M. Office of Works Committee for Bird Sanctuaries in Royal Parks.

76. Hudson had written nothing between 'very' and 'interest' which started a new page. I have added the word 'keen' which, I think, probably conveys what he intended.

77. In 1900 Hudson had initiated a campaign against the building of a national physical laboratory in the Old Deer Park. He wrote a letter of protest to *The Times* which was published on 14 April 1900: then the R.S.P.B. printed it as a leaflet and distributed it free of charge. It attracted a great deal of public support and was the first blow in a campaign which led to the cancellation of the project.

78. *Birds in London.*

79. The pamphlet for the (R.)S.P.B. entitled *Lost British Birds* (published as S.P.B. Pamphlet No. 14, *see* n. 45). Later he intended to expand this into a book, and had gathered much information and made extensive notes for this purpose. As indicated in this letter he never got around to it, so after his death Miss Linda Gardiner, the secretary of the R.S.P.B., collected and edited his notes, and they were published by Dent in book-form in 1923 as *Rare, Vanishing and Lost British Birds.*

PART TWO: LETTERS TO MRS EMMA HUBBARD AND
MRS ELIZA PHILLIPS

1. Ernest Hart (*see* also Letter 4) lived in Christchurch (now in Dorset). In 1894 he compiled a catalogue of birds and animals in the Hampshire Museum there.

2. Perhaps R. Bowdler Sharpe LL.D., FLS., etc. of the British Museum (in 1898 keeper, sub-department of vertebrata) who was a friend of Hudson's.

3. *The Birds of Sussex* by William Borrer (Porter, 1891).

4. The Zoological Society of London.

5. 'Wolmer Forest' by W. H. Hudson (*Longman's Magazine*, August 1897). Hudson re-used this article in Chapter X of his book *Hampshire Days* (Longmans, 1903).
6. Reverend John Edward ('Joey') Kelsall, MA., FZS., Rector of Milton from 1897 until his death at age 60 on 11 October 1924. He was well known as an ornithologist and, with P. W. Munn, wrote *Birds of Hampshire and the Isle of Wight* (Witherby, 1905).
7. Name omitted by editor.
8. Name omitted by editor. Same person as in Note 7.
9. Name omitted by editor. Same person as in Notes 7 and 8.
10. Probably Dr Alfred Russel Wallace who reviewed Hudson's book, *The Naturalist in La Plata*, in *Nature* of 14 April 1892. He called it, 'A remarkable book on the habits of animals', which, in his opinion, 'was altogether unique among books on natural history'. Hudson also mentions him in Chapter I of his book *Hampshire Days*, and in Chapter XIV of *Adventures Among Birds*.
11. Dr Cunningham Geikie of Bournemouth. In a letter to Edward Garnett on 15 April 1906 Hudson wrote of Geikie: 'Another old friend of mine who wrote the wisest, wittiest letters . . . died a few days ago — old Doctor Cunningham Geikie.' (*153 Letters from W. H. Hudson*, edited and introduced by Edward Garnett: Nonesuch Press, 1923.)
12. *See* Letter 3.
13. *See* Letter 1.
14. Evidently Hudson had taken Mrs Hubbard's gloves by mistake, but he was obviously jesting when he implied that he wore them, for his friends said he had large hands.
15. On page 136 of *British Birds* Hudson writes of the chaffinche's 'alarm-notes, usually spelt pink-pink or spink-spink, a clear penetrating sound, slightly metallic in character . . .'. Hudson had a remarkable knowledge of, and memory for, bird calls. For instance, 26 years after leaving Argentina he could still distinctly remember, or as he put it himself, 'reproduce in mind', the calls of 154 different species of Argentine birds. (*See* Chapter I of *Birds and Man*, 1901.)
16. Henry David Thoreau (1817–62), American writer, philosopher and naturalist.
17. This incident of drawing water in a tweed hat is related by Hudson in Chapter IX of *Nature in Downland*.
18. In Chapter VII of *Nature in Downland* Hudson writes about wheatears and of the shepherds formerly trapping them for sale as table delicacies.
19. To this letter Hudson had attached a pencilled sketch of this flower, under which he had written:
> 'Can you tell me what this flower is – natural size, very pure yellow fox-glovy in shape, with dark red spots on each petal.

I have seen one bed of it in the marsh: is it a British flower? I forget the name of the great tall plant that grows in the water with a profusion of purple-red composite flowers. It is just coming out now. The flowering rush has never grown here. The yellow loosestrife grows but is not in flower yet. There are acres of meadowsweet four or five feet high; and purple loosestrife and willow-herb, and a great deal of mullein on the roadside of the smaller kind with reddish brown inside.'

The flower which puzzled him was probably *Mimulus guttatus* (monkey flower) which he writes about in later letters. So perhaps Mrs Hubbard identified it for him.

20. Hudson omitted the date.
21. Probably Regent's Park.
22. Hudson's story of purchasing this bird for half-a-crown and releasing it in the Abbey Garden, Lewes, is related in R.S.P.B. Leaflet No. 73 entitled 'On Liberating Caged Birds', which was published in 1914.
23. Hudson relates this incident in Chapter XIX of *The Book of a Naturalist* (Hodder and Stoughton, 1919).
24. Richard Jefferies (1848–87), the Wiltshire-born writer who died at Goring on 14 August 1887. His grave is in Broadwater Cemetery, Worthing, where Hudson and his wife are also buried.
25. This is part of the same incident which Hudson related in Chapter I of *Nature in Downland* as follows:

> On a cloudy melancholy day in September I came in search of this cottage, and walking to the church by a narrow lane with a low trim wall-like hedge on either side, my thoughts were of Jefferies, who had doubtless often walked here, too, feeling the icy hand on him of one that walked invisible at his side. My mind was full of sadness, when, hearing the crunching of gravel beneath other feet than my own, I suddenly looked up, and behold, there before me stood the man himself, back on earth in the guise of a tramp. It was a most extraordinary coincidence that at such a moment I should have come face to face with this poor outcast and wanderer who had the Jefferies' countenance as I knew it from portraits and descriptions. It was the long thoughtfull suffering face, long straight nose, flowing brown beard, and rather large full blue eyes. I was startled at the expression, the unmistakable stamp of misery that was anguish and near to despair and insanity. He passed me, then paused, and after a moment or two said hesitatingly, 'Can you spare a penny?' I gave him something without looking at his face again, and went on my way sorry that I had met him, for I knew that those miserable eyes would continue to haunt me.

26. Near Slough in Buckinghamshire. Hudson and Mrs Hubbard had been planning an outing there.
27. Roydon House (now shown on the map as Roydon Manor) is midway between Brockenhurst and Boldre. Lymington was the postal address.
28. Hudson is referring to the long-tailed tit. 'Bottle' refers to its nest which he describes on page 92 of his *British Birds* as follows:
    > The nest is placed on a tree or bush, and is long in building, and a marvel of bird architecture. It is domed, oval in shape, with a small aperture near the top, and is composed of moss, lichens, and hair closely felted, and the interior thickly lined with feathers.'
29. *See* Letter 3.
30. Hudson included an account of the cuckoo clearing the nest in Chapter I of *Hampshire Days*.
31. Dr Alfred Russel Wallace (*see* also Letter 4).
32. *Birds from Moidart and Elsewhere* by Mrs Hugh Blackburn (David Douglas, 1895).
33. Doubtless Hudson is referring to the 'little liver pills' of that name.
34. Rollstone Farm, Fawley, Hampshire.
35. Gladstone bag.
36. *See* 'Introduction', Note 8. It was to Sir Edward Grey's cottage on the Itchen River at Itchen Abbas that Hudson had been invited.
37. Highwood House, at that time the ancestoral home of the Suckling family; now The Stroud School.
38. *See* Letter 11.
39. *See* Letter 11.
40. From Sir Edward Grey's cottage in which Hudson and his wife stayed from 21 July until the end of September 1900.
41. The word '(in)' has been inserted by the editor.
42. The word omitted was unreadable.
43. Secretary of the Edinburgh Branch of the (Royal) Society for the Protection of Birds: 'associates' would be associate members of that Society.
44. *British Birds*.
45. The whole of the name was unreadable but it was probably Sir Graham-Montgomery (Bart).
46. The (Royal) Society for the Protection of Birds.
47. The word omitted was unreadable.
48. Name omitted by the editor.
49. Mrs Frank Lemon, Honorary Secretary of the (Royal) Society for the Protection of Birds.
50. Author of *The Farmer's Boy*, a poem for which Hudson had a particular regard having chanced upon and purchased a copy from an old secondhand bookshop in Buenos Aires when a boy. Doubtless

this is the same 'small old forgotten book' to which he refers in this letter. Hudson devoted the whole of Chapter **XXIV** of his book *Afoot in England* (Hutchinson, 1909) to his visit to Troston (and associated places), Bloomfield and *The Farmer's Boy*.

51. Hudson had written 'Honiton' but undoubtedly intended 'Honington'.

52. Hudson related this story in Chapter **XXIII** of *Adventures Among Birds*.

53. The word omitted was unreadable.

54. The notepaper on which this letter was written was a rather dull depressing shade of green.

55. Now listed as lapwings.

TAILPIECE

1. From the private collection of Philip M. Correll, Esq.

2. *A Little Boy Lost* by W. H. Hudson (Duckworth, 1905).

Index

105

Selborne, 16, 73, 74
Selous, Edmund, 21
Serpentine River, 19, 56
Seven Sisters, the, 66
Shepherds, 66, 70, 72
Sherrington, 21
Sidmouth, 29
Smooth Snake, 76
Snipe, 20
Southampton, 73
Sparrow, 34
Sparrowhawk, 19, 44–45
Speaker, 53
Squirrel, 75
Star and Garter Home, 9
Starling, 34, 39, 71
Stoat, 49, 77
Story of my Heart, The, 43
Stratford Upon Avon, 72
Swallow, 16, 54, 65, 77, 82
Swift, 16, 37, 54–55

Tarle, Mrs, 72
Terry, Dame Ellen, 9
Terry, Fred, 9
Theatre, 9, 35, 36, 38, 51
Thetford, 28, 83
Thiselton-Dyer, Sir William, 27
Thomson, James, 33
Thoreau, Henry D., 65
Thrush, 26, 53, 71
Times, The 56
Tit, long-tailed or 'bottle', 71, 74
Trevor-Battye, A. B. R., 21
Troston, 83, 84
Turtle Dove, 39
Typhoon, 35

Victoria, Queen, 9

Vipers, 70
Vulture, 33

Wagtails, 30, 53, 66
Wallace, Dr A. R., 64, 72
Walsingham, Lord, 81
War (1914–18), 43
Warblers:
    Dartford, 8, 15, 20, 25, 28, 44, 73
    Marsh, 34, 36, 37, 52
Warminster, 22
Water Agrimony, 77
Wayside and Woodland Blossoms, 69
Weasel, 49
Wells, 22
Wells-next-the-sea, 29
West Sussex Downs, 75
Wheatears, 36, 66
Wheatley, Major, 56
Whitburn, Mr, 63
Willingdon, 69
Wimbledon Common, 27, 35
Wimborne, 22
Winchester, 76
Wolmer (Woolmer) Forest, 61, 62–63
Woodcocks, 71
Wood mouse, 77
Woodpeckers, 27, 35, 52, 55, 74, 75
Woolwich Common, 49
Worthing, 39, 46, 70, 71
Wrens, 73, 75
Wryneck, 34
Wylye River and Valley, 22

Yateley, 28

Zoological Gardens / Zoo (London),
    25, 30, 33, 39, 52
Zoological Society of London, 7, 62